TABE 11 & 12:
Full Study Guide and Test Strategies for the Test of Adult Basic Education

To obtain permission(s) to use the material from this work for any purpose including workshops or seminars, please submit a written request to

Smart Edition Media
36 Gorham Street
Suite 1
Cambridge, MA 02138
800-496-5994

Email: info@smarteditionmedia.com

Library of Congress Cataloging-in-Publication Data
Smart Edition Media.
TABE 11 & 12: Full Study Guide and Test Strategies for the Test of Adult Basic Education/Smart Edition Media.

ISBN: 978-1-949147-07-0, 1st edition

1. TABE 11 & 12
2. Study Guides
3. Test of Adult Basic Education
4. Adult Education
5. Career Training

Disclaimer:

The opinions expressed in this publication are the sole works of Smart Edition Media and were created independently from any National Evaluation Systems or other testing affiliates. Between the time of publication and printing, specific standards as well as testing formats and website information may change that are not included in part or in whole within this product. Smart Edition Media develops sample test questions, and they reflect similar content as on real tests; however, they are not former tests. Smart Edition Media assembles content that aligns with exam standards but makes no claims nor guarantees candidates a passing score.

Printed in the United States of America

TABE 11 & 12: Full Study Guide and Test Strategies for the Test of Adult Basic Education/Smart Edition Media.

ISBN: Print 978-1-949147-07-0
        Ebook 978-1-949147-08-7

TABE PRACTICE ONLINE

Smart Edition Media's Online Learning Resources allow you the flexibility to study for your exam on your own schedule and are the perfect companion to help you reach your goals! You

can access online content with an Internet connection from any computer, laptop, or mobile device.

Online Learning Resources

Designed to enable you to master the content in quick bursts of focused learning, these tools cover a complete range of subjects, including:

- English Language Arts
- Reading
- Math
- Science
- Writing

Our online resources are filled with test-taking tips and strategies, important facts, and practice problems that mirror questions on the exam.

Online Sample Tests & Flashcards

Access additional full-length practice tests online!

Use these tests as a diagnostic tool to determine areas of strength and weakness before embarking on your study program or to assess mastery of skills once you have completed your studies.

FLASHCARDS **GAMES** **QUIZZES** **TESTS**

Go to the URL: **https://smarteditionmedia.com/pages/tabe-online-resources** and follow the password/login instructions.

TABLE OF CONTENTS

Introduction

Test of Adult Basic Education (TABE) Overview

The Test of Adult Basic Education (TABE) is a standardized exam that measures academic skills commonly found in Adult Basic Education programs. The TABE is often used by adult education school administrators to assess the appropriate level of instruction required for incoming students. It is also used by employers as a tool to identify an employee's skills and abilities to tailor career training programs as a means to advance their career.

The skills included in the TABE are aligned with the College and Career Readiness standards outlined by the U.S. Department of Education and comply with Workforce Innovation and Opportunity Act (WIOA) regulations.

About This Book

This book provides you with an accurate and complete representation of the Test of Adult Basic Education (TABE) and includes all three sections found on the exam: Reading, Mathematics, and Language Arts. The reviews in this book are designed to provide the information and strategies you need to do well on the exam. The full-length practice test in the book is based on the TABE and contains questions similar to those you can expect to encounter on the official test. A detailed answer key follows each practice quiz and test. These answer keys provide explanations designed to help you completely understand the test material. Each explanation references the book chapter to allow you to go back to that section for additional review, if necessary.

Online Sample Tests

The purchase of this book grants you access to two additional full-length practice tests online. You can locate these exams on the Smart Edition Media website. Go to the URL: https://smarteditionmedia.com/pages/tabe-online-resources and follow the password/login instructions.

HOW TO USE THIS BOOK

Studies show that most people begin preparing for college-entry exams approximately 8 weeks before their test date. If you are scheduled to take your test in sooner than 8 weeks, do not despair! Smart Edition Media has designed this study guide to be flexible to allow you to concentrate on areas where you need the most support.

Whether you have 8 weeks to study – or much less than that – we urge you to take one of the online practice tests to determine areas of strength and weakness, if you have not done so already. These tests can be found in your online resources.

Once you have completed a practice test, use this information to help you create a study plan that suits your individual study habits and time frame. If you are short on time, look at your diagnostic test results to determine which subject matter could use the most attention and focus the majority of your efforts on those areas. While this study guide is organized to follow the order of the actual test, you are not required to complete the book from beginning to end, in that exact order.

HOW THIS BOOK IS ORGANIZED

Take a look at the Table of Contents. Notice that each **Section** in the study guide corresponds to a subtest of the exam. These sections are broken into **Chapters** that identify the major content categories of the exam.

Each chapter is further divided into individual **Lessons** that address the specific content and objectives required to pass the exam. Some lessons contain embedded example questions to assess your comprehension of the content "in the moment." All lessons contain a bulleted list called "**Let's Review**." Use this list to refresh your memory before taking a practice quiz, test, or the actual exam. A **Practice Quiz**, designed to check your progress as you move through the content, follows each chapter.

Whether you plan on working through the study guide from cover to cover, or selecting specific sections to review, each chapter of this book can be completed in one sitting. If you must end your study session before finishing a chapter, try to complete your current lesson in order to maximize comprehension and retention of the material.

ONLINE SAMPLE TESTS

The purchase of this book grants you access to two additional full-length practice tests online. You can locate these exams on the Smart Edition Media website.

STUDY STRATEGIES AND TIPS

MAKE STUDY SESSIONS A PRIORITY.

- Use a calendar to schedule your study sessions. Set aside a dedicated amount of time each day/week for studying. While it may seem difficult to manage, given your other responsibilities, remember that in order to reach your goals, it is crucial to dedicate the time now to prepare for this test. A satisfactory score on your exam is the key to unlocking a multitude of opportunities for your future success.
- Do you work? Have children? Other obligations? Be sure to take these into account when creating your schedule. Work around them to ensure that your scheduled study sessions can be free of distractions.

> **TIPS FOR FINDING TIME TO STUDY.**
> - Wake up 1-2 hours before your family for some quiet time
> - Study 1-2 hours before bedtime and after everything has quieted down
> - Utilize weekends for longer study periods
> - Hire a babysitter to watch children

TAKE PRACTICE TESTS

- Smart Edition Media offers practice tests, both online and in print. Take as many as you can to help be prepared. This will eliminate any surprises you may encounter during the exam.

KNOW YOUR LEARNING STYLE

- Identify your strengths and weaknesses as a student. All students are different and everyone has a different learning style. Do not compare yourself to others.
- Howard Gardner, a developmental psychologist at Harvard University, has studied the ways in which people learn new information. He has identified seven distinct intelligences. According to his theory:

  "we are all able to know the world through language, logical-mathematical analysis, spatial representation, musical thinking, the use of the body to solve problems or to make things, an understanding of other individuals, and an understanding of ourselves. Where individuals differ is in the strength of these intelligences - the so-called profile of intelligences -and in the ways in which such intelligences are invoked and combined to carry out different tasks, solve diverse problems, and progress in various domains."

- Knowing your learning style can help you to tailor your studying efforts to suit your natural strengths.
- What ways help you learn best? Videos? Reading textbooks? Find the best way for you to study and learn/review the material.

WHAT IS YOUR LEARNING STYLE?

- **Visual-Spatial** – Do you like to draw, do jigsaw puzzles, read maps, daydream? Creating drawings, graphic organizers, or watching videos might be useful for you.
- **Bodily-kinesthetic** – Do you like movement, making things, physical activity? Do you communicate well through body language, or like to be taught through physical activity? Hands-on learning, acting out, role playing are tools you might try.
- **Musical** – Do you show sensitivity to rhythm and sound? If you love music, and are also sensitive to sounds in your environments, it might be beneficial to study with music in the background. You can turn lessons into lyricsor speak rhythmically to aid in content retention.
- **Interpersonal** – Do you have many friends, empathy for others, street smarts, and interact well with others? You might learn best in a group setting. Form a study group with other students who are preparing for the same exam. Technology makes it easy to connect, if you are unable to meet in person, teleconferencing or video chats are useful tools to aid interpersonal learners in connecting with others.
- **Intrapersonal** – Do you prefer to work alone rather than in a group? Are you in tune with your inner feelings, follow your intuition and possess a strong will, confidence and opinions? Independent study and introspection will be ideal for you. Reading books, using creative materials, keeping a diary of your progress will be helpful. Intrapersonal learners are the most independent of the learners.
- **Linguistic** – Do you use words effectively, have highly developed auditory skills and often think in words? Do you like reading, playing word games, making up poetry or stories? Learning tools such as computers, games, multimedia will be beneficial to your studies.
- **Logical-Mathematical** – Do you think conceptually, abstractly, and are able to see and explore patterns and relationships? Try exploring subject matter through logic games, experiments and puzzles.

CREATE THE OPTIMAL STUDY ENVIRONMENT

- Some people enjoy listening to soft background music when they study. (Instrumental music is a good choice.) Others need to have a silent space in order to concentrate. Which do you prefer? Either way, it is best to create an environment that is free of distractions for your study sessions.
- Have study guide – Will travel! Leave your house: Daily routines and chores can be distractions. Check out your local library, a coffee shop, or other quiet space to remove yourself from distractions and daunting household tasks will compete for your attention.
- Create a Technology Free Zone. Silence the ringer on your cell phone and place it out of reach to prevent surfing the Web, social media interactions, and email/texting exchanges. Turn off the television, radio, or other devices while you study.
- Are you comfy? Find a comfortable, but not *too* comfortable, place to study. Sit at a desk or table in a straight, upright chair. Avoid sitting on the couch, a bed, or in front of the TV. Wear clothing that is not binding and restricting.
- Keep your area organized. Have all the materials you need available and ready: Smart Edition study guide, computer, notebook, pen, calculator, and pencil/eraser. Use a desk lamp or overhead light that provides ample lighting to prevent eye-strain and fatigue.

HEALTHY BODY, HEALTHY MIND

- Consider these words of wisdom from Buddha, "To keep the body in good health is a duty – otherwise we shall not be able to keep our mind strong and clear."

KEYS TO CREATING A HEALTHY BODY AND MIND:

- Drink water – Stay hydrated! Limit drinks with excessive sugar or caffeine.
- Eat natural foods – Make smart food choices and avoid greasy, fatty, sugary foods.
- Think positively – You can do this! Do not doubt yourself, and trust in the process.
- Exercise daily – If you have a workout routine, stick to it! If you are more sedentary, now is a great time to begin! Try yoga or a low-impact sport. Simply walking at a brisk pace will help to get your heart rate going.
- Sleep well – Getting a good night's sleep is important, but too few of us actually make it a priority. Aim to get eight hours of uninterrupted sleep in order to maximize your mental focus, memory, learning, and physical wellbeing.

FINAL THOUGHTS

- Remember to relax and take breaks during study sessions.
- Review the testing material. Go over topics you already know for a refresher.
- Focus more time on less familiar subjects.

EXAM PREPARATION

In addition to studying for your upcoming exam, it is important to keep in mind that you need to prepare your mind and body as well. When preparing to take an exam as a whole, not just studying, taking practice exams, and reviewing math rules, it is critical to prepare your body in order to be mentally and physically ready. Often, your success rate will be much higher when you are *fully* ready.

Here are some tips to keep in mind when preparing for your exam:

SEVERAL WEEKS/DAYS BEFORE THE EXAM

- Get a full night of sleep, approximately 8 hours
- Turn off electronics before bed
- Exercise regularly
- Eat a healthy balanced diet, include fruits and vegetable
- Drink water

THE NIGHT BEFORE

- Eat a good dinner
- Pack materials/bag, healthy snacks, and water

- Gather materials needed for test: your ID and receipt of test. You do not want to be scrambling the morning of the exam. If you are unsure of what to bring with you, check with your testing center or test administrator.
- Map the location of test center, identify how you will be getting there (driving, public transportation, uber, etc.), when you need to leave, and parking options.
- Lay your clothes out. Wear comfortable clothes and shoes, do not wear items that are too hot/cold
- Allow minimum of ~8 hours of sleep
- Avoid coffee and alcohol
- Do not take any medications or drugs to help you sleep
- Set alarm

THE DAY OF THE EXAM

- Wake up early, allow ample time to do all the things you need to do and for travel
- Eat a healthy, well-rounded breakfast
- Drink water
- Leave early and arrive early, leave time for any traffic or any other unforeseeable circumstances
- Arrive early and check in for exam. This will give you enough time to relax, take off coat, and become comfortable with your surroundings.

Take a deep breath, get ready, go! You got this!

SECTION I. LANGUAGE

Chapter 1 Conventions of Standard English

Spelling

Spelling correctly is important to accurately convey thoughts to an audience. This lesson will cover (1) vowels and consonants, (2) suffixes and plurals, (3) homophones and homographs.

Vowels and Consonants

Vowels and **consonants** are different speech sounds in English.

The letters A, E, I, O, U and sometimes Y are **vowels** and can create a variety of sounds. The most common are short sounds and long sounds. Long **vowel** sounds sound like the name of the letter such as the *a* in late. Short **vowel** sounds have a unique sound such as the *a* in cat. A rule for **vowels** is that when two vowels are walking, the first does the talking as in pain and meat.

Consonants include the other twenty-one letters in the alphabet. **Consonants** are weak letters and only make sounds when paired with **vowels**. That is why words always must have a **vowel**. This also means that **consonants** need to be doubled to make a stronger sound like sitting, grabbed, progress. Understanding general trends and patterns for **vowels** and **consonants** will help with spelling. The table below represents the difference between short and long **vowels** and gives examples for each.

	Symbol	Example Words
Short a	a	Cat, mat, hat, pat
Long a	ā	Late, pain, pay, they, weight, straight
Short e	e	Met, said, bread
Long e	ē	Breeze, cheap, dean, equal
Short i	i	Bit, myth, kiss, rip
Long i	ī	Cry, pie, high
Short o	o	Dog, hot, pop
Long o	ō	Snow, nose, elbow
Short u	u	Run, cut, club, gum
Long u	ū	Duty, rule, new, food
Short oo	oo	Book, foot, cookie
Long oo	ōō	Mood, bloom, shoot

Why isn't the word *pumpkin* a noun in the first sentence? *Pumpkin* is often a noun, but here it is used as an adjective that describes what kind of *pie*.

Why isn't the word *water* a noun in the second sentence? Here, *water* is an **action verb**. To *water the garden* is something we do.

How is the word *love* a noun in the third sentence and not in the fourth sentence? *Love* is a noun (thing) in sentence 3 and a verb (action) in the sentence 4.

How many nouns can a sentence contain? As long as the sentence remains grammatically correct, it can contain an unlimited number of nouns.

> **BE CAREFUL!**
> Words can change to serve different roles in different sentences. A word that is usually a noun can sometimes be used as an adjective or a verb. Determine a word's function in a sentence to be sure of its part of speech.

Types of Nouns

Singular and Plural Nouns

Nouns can be **singular** or **plural**. A noun is singular when there is only one. A noun is plural when there are two or more.

- The book has 650 pages.

Book is a singular noun. *Pages* is a plural noun.

Often, to make a noun plural, we add -*s* at the end of the word: *cat/cats*. This is a **regular** plural noun. Sometimes we make a word plural in another way: *child/children*. This is an **irregular** plural noun. Some plurals follow rules, while others do not. The most common rules are listed here:

> **KEEP IN MIND . . .**
> **Some nouns are countable,** and others are not. For example, we eat *three blueberries*, but we **do not** drink *three milks*. Instead, we drink *three glasses of milk* or *some milk*.

Singular noun	Plural noun	Rule for making plural
star	stars	for most words, add -*s*
box	boxes	for words that end in -*j*, -*s*, -*x*, -*z*, -*ch* or -*sh*, add -*es*
baby	babies	for words that end in -*y*, change -*y* to -*i* and add -*es*
woman	women	irregular
foot	feet	irregular

Common and Proper Nouns

Common nouns are general words, and they are written in lowercase. **Proper nouns** are specific names, and they begin with an uppercase letter.

PRONOUNS

A pronoun is a word that takes the place of or refers to a specific noun. This lesson will cover (1) the role of pronouns in sentences and (2) the purpose of pronouns.

Pronouns and Their Role in Sentences

A **pronoun** takes the place of a noun or refers to a specific noun.

Subject, Object, and Possessive Pronouns

A pronoun's role in a sentence is as **subject, object,** or **possessive**.

Subject Pronouns	Object Pronouns	Possessive Pronouns
I	me	my, mine
you	you	your, yours
he	her	his
she	him	her, hers
it	it	its
we	us	ours
they	them	their, theirs

In simple sentences, subject pronouns come before the verb, object pronouns come after the verb, and possessive pronouns show ownership.

Look at the pronouns in these examples:

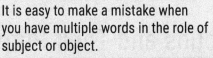

BE CAREFUL!

It is easy to make a mistake when you have multiple words in the role of subject or object.

- <u>She</u> forgot <u>her</u> coat. (subject: she; possessive: her)
- <u>I</u> lent <u>her</u> <u>mine</u>. (subject: I; object: her; possessive: mine)
- <u>She</u> left <u>it</u> at school. (subject: she; object: it)
- <u>I</u> had to go and get <u>it</u> the next day. (subject: I; object: it)
- <u>I</u> will never lend <u>her</u> something of <u>mine</u> again! (subject: I; object: her; possessive: mine)

Correct	Incorrect	Why?
John and I went out.	*John and me* went out.	*John and I* is a subject. *I* is a subject pronoun; *me* is not.
Johan took *Sam and me* to the show.	Johan took *Sam and I* to the show.	*Sam and me* is an object. *Me* is an object pronoun; *I* is not.

Relative Pronouns

Relative pronouns connect a clause to a noun or pronoun.

These are some relative pronouns:

who, whom, whoever, whose, that, which

- Steve Jobs, *who founded Apple*, changed the way people use technology.

The pronoun *who* introduces a clause that gives more information about Steve Jobs.

- This is the movie *that Emily told us to see.*

The pronoun *that* introduces a clause that gives more information about the movie.

Other Pronouns

Some other pronouns are:

this, that, what, anyone, everything, something

> **DID YOU KNOW?**
> Pronouns can sometimes refer to general or unspecified things.

Look for the pronouns in these sentences.

- What is that?
- There is something over there!
- Does anyone have a pen?

Pronouns and Their Purpose

The purpose of a pronoun is to replace a noun. Note the use of the pronoun *their* in the heading of this section. If we did not have pronouns, we would have to call this section *Pronouns and Pronouns' Purpose.*

What Is an Antecedent?

A pronoun in a sentence refers to a specific noun, and this noun called the **antecedent**.

- John Hancock signed the Declaration of Independence. <u>He</u> signed <u>it</u> in 1776.

The antecedent for *he* is John Hancock.
The antecedent for *it* is the Declaration of Independence.

> **BE CAREFUL!**
> Look out for unclear antecedents, such as in this sentence:
>
> - Take the furniture out of the room and paint *it*.
>
> What needs to be painted, the furniture or the room?

Find the pronouns in the following sentence. Then identify the antecedent for each pronoun.

Erin had an idea *that she* suggested to Antonio: "*I*'ll help *you* with *your* math homework if *you* help *me* with *my* writing assignment."

Pronoun	Antecedent
that	idea
she	Erin
I	Erin
you	Antonio
your	Antonio's
you	Antonio
me	Erin
my	Erin's

What Is Antecedent Agreement?

A pronoun must agree in **gender** and **number** with the antecedent it refers to. For example:

- Singular pronouns *I, you, he, she,* and *it* replace singular nouns.
- Plural pronouns *you, we,* and *they* replace plural nouns.
- Pronouns *he, she,* and *it* replace masculine, feminine, or neutral nouns.

Correct	Incorrect	Why?
Students should do their homework every night.	A student should do their homework every night.	The pronoun *their* is plural, so it must refer to a plural noun such as *students*.
When an employee is sick, he or she should call the office.	When an employee is sick, they should call the office.	The pronoun *they* is plural, so it must refer to a plural noun. *Employee* is not a plural noun.

Let's Review!

- A pronoun takes the place of or refers to a noun.
- The role of pronouns in sentences is as subject, object, or possessive.
- A pronoun must agree in number and gender with the noun it refers to.

ADJECTIVES AND ADVERBS

An **adjective** is a word that describes a noun or a pronoun. An **adverb** is a word that describes a verb, an adjective, or another adverb.

Adjectives

An **adjective** describes, modifies, or tells us more about a **noun** or a **pronoun**. Colors, numbers, and descriptive words such as *healthy, good,* and *sharp* are adjectives.

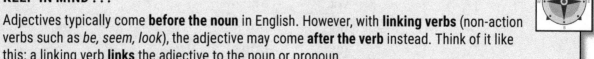

KEEP IN MIND . . .
Adjectives typically come **before the noun** in English. However, with **linking verbs** (non-action verbs such as *be, seem, look*), the adjective may come **after the verb** instead. Think of it like this: a linking verb **links** the adjective to the noun or pronoun.

Look for the adjectives in the following sentences:

	Adjective	Noun or pronoun it describes
I rode the blue bike.	blue	bike
It was a long trip.	long	trip
Bring two pencils for the exam.	two	pencils
The box is brown.	brown	box
She looked beautiful.	beautiful	she
That's great!	great	that

Multiple adjectives can be used in a sentence, as can multiple nouns. Look at these examples:

	Adjectives	Noun or pronoun it describes
The six girls were happy, healthy, and rested after their long beach vacation.	six, happy, healthy, rested; long, beach	girls; vacation
Leo has a good job, but he is applying for a better one.	good; better	job; one

KEEP IN MIND . . .
Note comparative and superlative forms of adjectives, such as:

fast, faster, fastest

far, farther, farthest

good, better, best

bad, worse, worst

Articles: *A, An, The*

Articles are a unique part of speech, but they work like adjectives. An article tells more about a noun. *A* and *an* are **indefinite** articles. Use *a* before a singular **general** noun. Use *an* before a singular general noun that begins with a vowel.

The is a **definite** article. Use *the* before a singular or plural **specific** noun.

Look at how articles are used in the following sentences:

- I need *a* pencil to take *the* exam. (any pencil; specific exam)
- Is there *a* zoo in town? (any zoo)
- Let's go to *the* zoo today. (specific zoo)
- Can you get me *a* glass of milk? (any glass)
- Would you bring me *the* glass that's over there? (specific glass)

Adverbs

An **adverb** describes, modifies, or tells us more about a **verb**, an **adjective**, or another **adverb**. Many adverbs end in *-ly*. Often, adverbs tell when, where, or how something happened. Words such as *slowly, very,* and *yesterday* are adverbs.

Adverbs that Describe Verbs

Adverbs that describe verbs tell something more about the action.

Look for the adverbs in these sentences:

	Adverb	Verb it describes
They walked quickly.	quickly	walked
She disapproved somewhat of his actions, but she completely understood them.	somewhat; completely	disapproved; understood
The boys will go inside if it rains heavily.	inside; heavily	go; rains

Adverbs that Describe Adjectives

Adverbs that describe adjectives often add intensity to the adjective. Words like *quite, more,* and *always* are adverbs.

Look for the adverbs in these sentences:

	Adverb	Adjective it describes
The giraffe is very tall.	very	tall
Do you think that you are more intelligent than them?	more	intelligent
If it's really loud, we can make the volume slightly lower.	really; slightly	loud; lower

CHAPTER 2 PARTS OF SPEECH
PRACTICE QUIZ — ANSWER KEY

1. **B.** *Quite* is an adverb that describes the adverb *well*. **See Lesson: Adjectives and Adverbs.**

2. **D.** These adjectives describe *Henry*. **See Lesson: Adjectives and Adverbs.**

3. **D.** *Wisely* is an adverb that describes the verb *spoke*. **See Lesson: Adjectives and Adverbs.**

4. **B.** *Yet* is a conjunction. **See Lesson: Conjunctions and Prepositions.**

5. **A.** *Keep me informed* does not contain a preposition. *About, of,* and *throughout* are prepositions. **See Lesson: Conjunctions and Prepositions.**

6. **D.** *From, to,* and *for* are prepositions. **See Lesson: Conjunctions and Prepositions.**

7. **B.** *Matthew* and *Tuesday* are proper nouns. **See Lesson: Nouns.**

8. **A.** *Marie's* and *father's* are possessive; neither is plural. *Appendix* is a singular noun. **See Lesson: Nouns.**

9. **D.** *Health* is an abstract noun; it does not physically exist. **See Lesson: Nouns.**

10. **C.** *Whom* is a pronoun. **See Lesson: Pronouns.**

11. **B.** An object pronoun must be used here. **See Lesson: Pronouns.**

12. **D.** *Who* is a relative pronoun that refers to the subject *Greta Garbo*. **See Lesson: Pronouns.**

13. **C.** *Toured* and *saw* are verbs. **See Lesson: Verbs and Verb Tenses.**

14. **A.** *Did* is a helping verb; *ask* is the main verb. **See Lesson: Verbs and Verb Tenses.**

15. **B.** *Did* can be used here, for a shortened form of *did enjoy it*. **See Lesson: Verbs and Verb Tenses.**

CHAPTER 3 KNOWLEDGE OF LANGUAGE

TYPES OF SENTENCES

Sentences are a combination of words that communicate a complete thought. Sentences can be written in many ways to signal different relationships among ideas. This lesson will cover (1) simple sentences (2) compound sentences (3) complex sentences (4) parallel structure.

Simple Sentences

A **simple sentence** is a group of words that make up a **complete thought**. To be a complete thought, simple sentences must have one **independent clause.** An independent clause contains a single **subject** (who or what the sentence is about) and a **predicate** (a **verb** and something about the subject.)

Let's take a look at some simple sentences:

Simple Sentence	Subject	Predicate	Complete Thought?
The car was fast.	car	was fast (verb = was)	Yes
Sally waited for the bus.	Sally	waited for the bus (verb = waited)	Yes
The pizza smells delicious.	pizza	smells delicious (verb = smells)	Yes
Anton loves cycling.	Anton	loves cycling (verb = loves)	Yes

It is important to be able to recognize what a simple sentence is in order to avoid **run-ons** and **fragments**, two common grammatical errors.

A **run-on** is when two or more independent clauses are combined without proper punctuation:

FOR EXAMPLE

Gregory is a very talented actor he was the lead in the school play.

If you take a look at this sentence, you can see that it is made up of 2 independent clauses or simple sentences:

1. *Gregory is a very talented actor*
2. *he was the lead in the school play*

You <u>cannot</u> have two independent clauses running into each other without proper punctuation.

You can fix this run-on in the following way:

Gregory is a very talented actor. He was the lead in the school play.

A **fragment** is a group of words that looks like a sentence. It starts with a capital letter and has end punctuation, but when you examine it closely you will see it is not a complete thought.

Let's put this information all together to determine whether a group of words is a simple sentence, a run-on, or a fragment:

Group of Words	Category
Mondays are the worst they are a drag.	Run-On: These are two independent clauses running into one another without proper punctuation. FIX: *Mondays are the worst. They are a drag.*
Because I wanted soda.	Fragment: This is a dependent clause and needs more information to make it a complete thought. FIX: *I went to the store because I wanted soda.*
Ereni is from Greece.	Simple Sentence: YES! This is a simple sentence with a subject (*Ereni*) and a predicate (*is from Greece*), so it is a complete thought.
While I was apple picking.	Fragment: This is a dependent clause and needs more information to make it a complete thought. FIX: *While I was apple picking, I spotted a bunny.*
New York City is magical it is my favorite place.	Run-On: These are two independent clauses running into one another without proper punctuation. FIX: *New York City is magical. It is my favorite place.*

Compound Sentences

A **compound sentence** is a sentence made up of two independent clauses connected with a **coordinating conjunction**.

Let's take a look at the following sentence:

Joe waited for the bus, but it never arrived.

If you take a close look at this compound sentence, you will see that it is made up of two independent clauses:

1. *Joe waited for the bus*
2. *it never arrived*

The word *but* is the coordinating conjunction that connects these two sentences. Notice that the coordinating conjunction has a comma right before it. This is the proper way to punctuate compound sentences.

Here are other examples of compound sentences:

FOR EXAMPLE

I want to try out for the baseball team, and I also want to try out for track.

*Sally can play the clarinet in the band, **or** she can play the violin in the orchestra.*

*Mr. Henry is going to run the half marathon, **so** he has a lot of training to do.*

All these sentences are compound sentences since they each have two independent clauses joined by a comma and a coordinating conjunction.

The following is a list of **coordinating conjunctions** that can be used in compound sentences. You can use the mnemonic device "FANBOYS" to help you remember them:

For

And

Nor

But

Or

Yet

So

Think back to Section 1: Simple Sentences. You learned about run-ons. Another way to fix run-ons is by turning the group of words into a compound sentence:

RUN-ON:	*Gregory is a very talented actor he was the lead in the school play.*
FIX:	*Gregory is a very talented actor,* **so** *he was the lead in the school play.*

Complex Sentences

A **complex** sentence is a sentence that is made up of an independent clause and one or more dependent clauses connected to it.

Think back to Section 1 when you learned about fragments. You learned about a **dependent clause**, the part of a sentence that cannot stand by itself. These clauses need other information to make them complete.

You can recognize a dependent clause because they always begin with a **subordinating conjunction**. These words are a key ingredient in complex sentences.

Here is a list of **subordinating conjunctions:**

after	although	as	because	before
despite	even if	even though	if	in order to
that	once	provided that	rather than	since
so that	than	that	though	unless
until	when	whenever	where	whereas
wherever	while	why		

Let's take a look at a few complex sentences:

> **FOR EXAMPLE**
>
> ***Since the alarm clock didn't go off, I was late for class.***
>
> This is an example of a complex sentence because it contains:
>
> A dependent clause: *Since the alarm clock didn't go off*
> An independent clause: *I was late for class*
> A subordinating conjunction: *since*
>
> ***Sarah studied all night for the exam even though she did not receive an A.***
>
> This is an example of a complex sentence because it contains:
>
> A dependent clause: *even though she did not receive an A*
> An independent clause: *Sarah studied all night*
> A subordinating conjunction: *even though*
>
> ***NOTE:*** *To make a complex sentence, you can either start with the dependent clause or the independent clause. When beginning with the dependent clause, you need a comma after it. When beginning with an independent clause, you do not need a comma after it.*

Parallel Structure

Parallel structure is the repetition of a grammatical form within a sentence to make the sentence sound more harmonious. Parallel structure comes into play when you are making a list of items. Stylistically, you want all the items in the list to line up with each other to make them sound better.

Let's take a look at when to use parallel structure:

1. Use parallel structure with verb forms:

    In a sentence listing different verbs, you want all the verbs to use the same form:

    Manuel likes hiking, biking, and mountain climbing.

    In this example, the words *hiking, biking* and *climbing* are all gerunds (having an -ing ending), so the sentence is balanced since the words are all using the gerund form of the verb.

    Manuel likes to hike, bike, and mountain climb.

In this example, the words *hike, bike* and *climb* are all infinitives (using the basic form of the verb), so the sentence is balanced.

You do not want to mix them up:

Manuel likes hiking, biking, and to mountain climb.

This sentence **does not** use parallel structure since *hiking* and *biking* use the gerund form of the verb and *to mountain climb* uses the infinitive form.

2. Use parallel structure with active and passive voice:

In a sentence written in the **active voice**, the subject performs the action:

Sally kicked the ball.

Sally, the subject, is the one doing the action, kicking the ball.

In a sentence written in the **passive voice**, the subject is acted on by the verb.

The ball was kicked by Sally.

When using parallel structure, you want to make sure your items in a list are either all in **active voice**:

Raymond baked, frosted, and decorated the cake.

Or all in **passive voice**:

The cake was baked, frosted, and decorated by Raymond.

You do not want to mix them up:

The cake was baked, frosted, and Raymond decorated it.

This sentence **does not** use parallel structure because it starts off with passive voice and then switches to active voice.

3. Use parallel structure with the length of terms within a list:

When making a list, you should either have all short individual terms or all long phrases.

Keep these consistent by either choosing short, individual terms:

Cassandra is bold, courageous, and strong.

Or longer phrases:

Cassandra is brave in the face of danger, willing to take risks, and a force to be reckoned with.

You do not want to mix them up:

Cassandra is bold, courageous, and a force to be reckoned with.

This sentence **does not** use parallel structure because the first two terms are short, and the last one is a longer phrase.

Let's Review!

- A simple sentence consists of a clause, which has a single subject and a predicate.
- A compound sentence is made up of two independent clauses connected by a coordinating conjunction.
- A complex sentence is made up of a subordinating conjunction, an independent clause and one or more dependent clauses connected to it.
- Parallel structure is the repetition of a grammatical form within a sentence to make the sentence sound more harmonious.

CHAPTER 3 KNOWLEDGE OF LANGUAGE PRACTICE QUIZ

1. **Identify the direct object in the following sentence.**

   Paulo accidentally locked his keys in his car.

   A. Paulo   C. his keys

   B. accidentally   D. his car

2. **Select the word that is an object of the underlined verb.**

   The graduates <u>held</u> lit candles.

   A. The   C. lit

   B. graduates   D. candles

3. **Select the verb that acts on the underlined direct object in the following sentence.**

   We have no choice but to sit here and wait for these cows to cross <u>the road</u>!

   A. have   C. wait

   B. sit   D. cross

4. **Which modifier, if any, modifies the underlined word in the following sentence?**

   We always visit the <u>bakery</u> on the corner when we are in town.

   A. always   C. when we are in town

   B. on the corner

        D. No modifier describes it.

5. **Identify the dangling or misplaced modifier, if there is one.**

   Having been repaired, we can drive the car again.

   A. Having been repaired

   B. we can drive

   C. the car again

   D. There is no dangling or misplaced modifier.

6. **Which ending does <u>not</u> create a sentence with a dangling modifier?**

   Trying to earn some extra money, ____.

   A. the new position paid more

   B. he got a second job

   C. the job was difficult

   D. it was an extra shift

7. **Select the "understood" subject with which the underlined verb must agree.**

   <u>Watch</u> out!

   A. You   C. I

   B. He   D. Out

8. **How many verbs must agree with the underlined subject in the following sentence?**

   <u>Kareem Abdul-Jabbar</u>, my favorite basketball player, dribbles, shoots, and scores to win the game!

   A. 0   C. 2

   B. 1   D. 3

9. **Select the correct verb to complete the following sentence.**

   Our family ____ staying home for the holidays this year.

   A. is
   B. be
   C. am
   D. are

10. **Fill in the blank with the correct subordinating conjunction.**

    You cannot go to the movies with your friends _____ you finish your homework.

    A. if
    B. once
    C. since
    D. unless

11. **Identify the dependent clause in the following sentence.**

    We decided to take our dog to the park although it was hot outside.

    A. We decided to take our dog
    B. to the park
    C. although it was hot outside
    D. to take our dog

12. **Identify the independent clause in the following sentence.**

    After eating dinner, the couple went on a stroll through the park.

    A. After eating dinner
    B. the couple went on a stroll through the park
    C. through the park
    D. went on a stroll

13. **Which of the following is an example of a simple sentence?**

    A. Tamara's sporting goods store.
    B. Tamara has a sporting goods store in town.
    C. Tamara has a sporting goods store it is in town.
    D. Tamara's sporting goods store is in town, and she is the owner.

14. **Which of the following uses a conjunction to combine the sentences below so the focus is on puppies requiring a lot of work?**

    Puppies are fun-loving animals. They do require a lot of work.

    A. Puppies are fun-loving animals; they do require a lot of work.
    B. Puppies are fun-loving animals, so they do require a lot of work.
    C. Since puppies are fun-loving animals they do require a lot of work.
    D. Although puppies are fun-loving animals, they do require a lot of work.

15. **Which of these options would complete the following sentence to make it a compound sentence?**

    The class of middle school students _____.

    A. served food at
    B. served food at a soup kitchen
    C. served food at a soup kitchen, and they enjoyed the experience
    D. served food at a soup kitchen even though they weren't required to

CHAPTER 3 KNOWLEDGE OF LANGUAGE PRACTICE QUIZ — ANSWER KEY

1. C. *His keys* is the direct object of the verb *locked*. **See Lesson: Direct Objects and Indirect Objects.**

2. D. *Candles* is the direct object of the verb *held*. **See Lesson: Direct Objects and Indirect Objects.**

3. D. *The road* is a direct object of the verb *cross*. **See Lesson: Direct Objects and Indirect Objects.**

4. B. *On the corner* modifies *bakery*. **See Lesson: Modifiers.**

5. A. *Having been repaired* is placed where it references *we*, but it should reference *the car*. **See Lesson: Modifiers.**

6. B. Of these choices, *trying to earn some extra money* can only reference *he*. **See Lesson: Modifiers.**

7. A. In a command like this one, the "understood" subject is *you*. **See Lesson: Subject and Verb Agreement.**

8. D. The verbs *dribbles, shoots,* and *scores* must agree with the subject *Kareem Abdul-Jabbar*. **See Lesson: Subject and Verb Agreement.**

9. A. The subject *family* is singular and takes the verb *is*. **See Lesson: Subject and Verb Agreement.**

10. D. The word "unless" signifies the beginning of a dependent clause and is the only conjunction that makes sense in the sentence. **See Lesson: Types of Clauses.**

11. C. *Although it was hot outside* is dependent because it does not express a complete thought and relies on the independent clause. The word "although" also signifies the beginning of a dependent clause. **See Lesson: Types of Clauses.**

12. B. The couple went on a stroll through the park. It is independent because it has a subject, verb, and expresses a complete thought. **See Lesson: Types of Clauses.**

13. B. This is a simple sentence since it contains one independent clause consisting of a simple subject and a predicate. **See Lesson: Types of Sentences.**

14. D. The subordinate conjunction "although" combines the sentences and puts the focus on puppies requiring a lot of work. **See Lesson: Types of Sentences.**

15. C. This option would make the sentence a compound sentence. **See Lesson: Types of Sentences.**

CHAPTER 4 VOCABULARY ACQUISITION

ROOT WORDS, PREFIXES, AND SUFFIXES

A root word is the most basic part of a word. You can create new words by: adding a prefix, a group of letters placed before the root word; or a suffix, a group of letters placed at the end of a root word. In this lesson you will learn about root words, prefixes, suffixes, and how to determine the meaning of a word by analyzing these word parts.

Root Words

Root words are found in everyday language. They are the most basic parts of words. Root words in the English language are mostly derived from Latin or Greek. You can add beginnings (prefixes) and endings (suffixes) to root words to change their meanings. To discover what a root word is, simply remove its prefix and/or suffix. What you are left with is the root word, or the core or basis of the word.

At times, root words can be stand-alone words.

Here are some examples of stand-alone root words:

Stand-Alone Root Word	Meaning
dress	*clothing*
form	*shape*
normal	*typical*
phobia	*fear of*
port	*carry*

Most root words, however, are **not** stand-alone words. They are not full words on their own, but they still form the basis of other words when you remove their prefixes and suffixes.

Here are some common root words in the English language:

Root Word	Meaning	Example
ami, amic	*love*	amicable
anni	*year*	anniversary
aud	*to hear*	auditory
bene	*good*	beneficial
biblio	*book*	bibliography
cap	*take, seize*	capture
cent	*one hundred*	century
chrom	*color*	chromatic

Root Word	Meaning	Example
chron	*time*	chronological
circum	*around*	circumvent
cred	*believe*	credible
corp	*body*	corpse
dict	*to say*	dictate
equi	*equal*	equality
fract; rupt	*to break*	fracture
ject	*throw*	eject
mal	*bad*	malignant
min	*small*	miniature
mort	*death*	mortal
multi	*many*	multiply
ped	*foot*	pedestrian
rupt	*break*	rupture
sect	*cut*	dissect
script	*write*	manuscript
sol	*sun*	solar
struct	*build*	construct
terr	*earth*	terrain
therm	*heat*	thermometer
vid, vis	*to see*	visual
voc	*voice; to call*	vocal

Prefixes

Prefixes are the letters added to the **beginning** of a root word to make a new word with a different meaning.

Prefixes on their own have meanings, too. If you add a prefix to a root word, it can change its meaning entirely.

Here are some of the most common prefixes, their meanings, and some examples:

Prefix	Meaning	Example
auto	*self*	autograph
con	*with*	conclude
hydro	*water*	hydrate
im, in, non, un	*not*	unimportant
inter	*between*	international
mis	*incorrect, badly*	mislead

Prefix	Meaning	Example
over	*too much*	over-stimulate
post	*after*	postpone
pre	*before*	preview
re	*again*	rewrite
sub	*under, below*	submarine
trans	*across*	transcribe

Let's look back at some of the root words from Section 1. By adding prefixes to these root words, you can create a completely new word with a new meaning:

Root Word	Prefix	New Word	Meaning
dress (*clothing*)	un (*remove*)	**un**dress	*remove clothing*
sect (*cut*)	inter (*between*)	**inter**sect	*cut across or through*
phobia (*fear*)	hydro (*water*)	**hydro**phobia	*fear of water*
script (*write*)	post (*after*)	**post**script	*additional remark at the end of a letter*

Suffixes

Suffixes are the letters added to the **end** of a root word to make a new word with a different meaning.

Suffixes on their own have meanings, too. If you add a suffix to a root word, it can change its meaning entirely.

Here are some of the most common suffixes, their meanings, and some examples:

Suffix	Meanings	Example
able, ible	*can be done*	agreeable
an, ean, ian	*belonging or relating to*	European
ed	*happened in the past*	jogged
en	*made of*	wooden
er	*comparative (more than)*	stricter
est	*comparative (most)*	largest
ful	*full of*	meaningful
ic	*having characteristics of*	psychotic
ion, tion, ation, ition	*act, process*	hospitalization
ist	*person who practices*	linguist
less	*without*	artless
logy	*study of*	biology

Let's look back at some of the root words from Section 1. By adding suffixes to these root words, you can create a completely new word with a new meaning:

Root Word	Suffix	New Word	Meaning
aud (*to hear*)	logy (*study of*)	audio**logy**	*the study of hearing*
form (*shape*)	less (*without*)	form**less**	*without a clear shape*
port (*carry*)	able (*can be done*)	port**able**	*able to be carried*
normal (*typical*)	ity (*state of*)	normal**ity**	*condition of being normal*

Determining Meaning

Knowing the meanings of common root words, prefixes, and suffixes can help you determine the meaning of unknown words. By looking at a word's individual parts, you can get a good sense of its definition.

If you look at the word *transportation*, you can study the different parts of the word to figure out what it means.

If you were to break up the word you would see the following:

PREFIX: *trans = across*	ROOT: *port = carry*	SUFFIX: *tion = act or process*

If you put all these word parts together, you can define transportation as: *the act or process of carrying something across.*

Let's define some other words by looking at their roots, prefixes and suffixes:

Word	Prefix	Root	Suffix	Working Definition
indestructible	in (*not*)	struct (*build*)	able (*can be done*)	Not able to be "un" built (torn down)
nonconformist	non (*not*) con (*with*)	form (*shape*)	ist (*person who practices*)	A person who can not be shaped (someone who doesn't go along with the norm)
subterranean	sub (*under, below*)	terr (*earth*)	ean (*belonging or relating to*)	Relating or belonging to something under the earth

Let's Review!

- A root word is the most basic part of a word.
- A prefix is the letters added to beginning of a root word to change the word and its meaning.
- A suffix is the letters added to the end of a root word to change the word and its meaning.
- You can figure out a word's meaning by looking closely at its different word parts (root, prefixes, and suffixes).

CONTEXT CLUES AND MULTIPLE MEANING WORDS

Sometimes when you read a text, you come across an unfamiliar word. Instead of skipping the word and reading on, it is important to figure out what that word means so you can better understand the text. There are different strategies you can use to determine the meaning of unfamiliar words. This lesson will cover (1) how to determine unfamiliar words by reading context clues, (2) multiple meaning words, and (3) using multiple meaning words properly in context.

Using Context Clues to Determine Meaning

When reading a text, it is common to come across unfamiliar words. One way to determine the meaning of unfamiliar words is by studying other context clues to help you better understand what the word means.

Context means the other words in the sentences around the unfamiliar word.

You can look at these other words to find **clues** or **hints** to help you figure out what the word means.

FOR EXAMPLE

Look at the following sentence:

Some of the kids in the cafeteria _ostracized_ Janice because she dressed differently; they never allowed her to sit at their lunch table, and they whispered behind her back.

If you did not know what the word _ostracized_ meant, you could look at the **other words** for **clues** to help you.

Here is what we know based on the clues in the sentence:

- Janice dressed differently
- Some kids did not allow her to sit at their table
- They whispered behind her back

We know that the kids **never allowed her to sit at their lunch** table and that they **whispered behind her back**. If you put all these clues together, you can conclude that the other students were **mistreating** Janice by **excluding** her.

Therefore, based on these context clues, _ostracized_ means "excluded from the group."

Here's another example:

EXAMPLE 2

Look at this next sentence:

Louis's teacher was offended because after she called on him he gave a *flippant* response instead of a serious answer.

If you did not know what the word *flippant* meant, you could look at the **other words** for **clues** to help you.

Here is what we know based on the clues in the sentence:

- Louis's teacher was offended
- He gave a flippant response instead of a serious answer

We know that Louis said something that **offended** his teacher. Another keyword in this sentence is the word **instead**. This means that **instead of a serious answer** Louis gave the **opposite** of a serious answer.

Therefore, based on these context clues, *flippant* means "lacking respect or seriousness."

Multiple Meaning Words

Sometimes when we read words in a text, we encounter words that have **multiple meanings**.

Multiple meaning words are words that have **more than one definition** or meaning.

FOR EXAMPLE

The word **current** is a multiple meaning word. Here are the different definitions of *current*:

CURRENT:

1. adj: happening or existing in the present time

    Example: *It is important to keep up with current events so you know what's happening in the world.*

2. noun: the continuous movement of a body of water or air in a certain direction

    Example: *The river's current was strong as we paddled down the rapids.*

3. noun: a flow of electricity

    Example: *The electrical current was very weak in the house.*

Here are some other examples of words with multiple meanings:

Multiple Meaning Word	Definition #1	Definition #2	Definition #3
Buckle	noun: a metal or plastic device that connects one end of a belt to another	verb: to fasten or attach	verb: to bend or collapse from pressure or heat
Cabinet	noun: a piece of furniture used for storing things	noun: a group of people who give advice to a government leader	-
Channel	noun: a radio or television station	noun: a system used for sending something	noun: a long, narrow place where water flows
Doctor	noun: a person skilled in the science of medicine, dentistry, or one holding a PhD	verb: to change something in a way to trick or deceive	verb: to give medical treatment
Grave	noun: a hole in the ground for burying a dead body	adj: very serious	-
Hamper	noun: a large basket used for holding dirty clothes	verb: to slow the movement, action, or progress of	-
Plane	noun: a mode of transportation that has wings and an engine and can carry people and things in the air	noun: a flat or level surface that extends outward	noun: a level of though, development, or existence
Reservation	noun: an agreement to have something (such as a table, room, or seat) held for use at a later time	noun: a feeling of uncertainty or doubt	noun: an area of land kept separate for Native Americans to live an area of land set aside for animals to live for protection
Season	noun: one of the four periods in which a year is divided (winter, spring, summer, and fall)	noun: a particular period of time during the year	verb: to add spices to something to give it more flavor
Sentence	noun: a group words that expresses a statement, question, command, or wish	noun: the punishment given to someone by a court of law	verb: to officially state the punishment given by a court of law

From this chart you will notice that words with multiple meanings may have different **parts of speech**. A part of speech is a category of words that have the same grammatical properties. Some of the main parts of speech for words in the English language are: nouns, adjectives, verbs, and adverbs.

Part of Speech	Definition	Example
Noun	a person, place, thing, or idea	*Linda, New York City, toaster, happiness*
Adjective	a word that describes a noun or pronoun	*adventurous, young, red, intelligent*
Verb	an action or state of being	*run, is, sleep, become*
Adverb	a word that describes a verb, adjective, or other adverb	*quietly, extremely, carefully, well*

For example, in the chart above, *season* can be a **noun** or a **verb**.

Using Multiple Meaning Words Properly in Context

When you come across a **multiple meaning word** in a text, it is important to discern which meaning of the word is being used so you do not get confused.

You can once again turn to the **context clues** to clarify which meaning of the word is being used.

Let's take a look at the word *coach*. This word has several definitions:

COACH:
1. noun: a person who teaches and trains an athlete or performer
2. noun: a large bus with comfortable seating used for long trips
3. noun: the section on an airplane with the least expensive seats
4. verb: to teach or train someone in a specific area
5. verb: to give someone instructions on what to do or say in a certain situation

Since *coach* has so many definitions, you need to look at the **context clues** to figure out which definition of the word is being used:

The man was not happy that he had to sit in coach on the 24-hour flight to Australia.

In this sentence, the context clues **sit in** and **24-hour flight** help you see that *coach* means the least expensive seat on an airplane.

Let's look at another sentence using the word *coach*:

The lawyer needed to coach her witness so he would answer all the questions properly.

In this sentence, the context clues **so he would answer all the questions properly** help you see that the lawyer was giving the witness instructions on what to say.

Let's Review!
- When you come across an unfamiliar word in a text you can use context clues to help you define it.
- Context clues can also help you determine which definition of a multiple meaning word to use.

SYNONYMS, ANTONYMS, AND ANALOGIES

In order to utilize language to the best of your ability while reading, writing, or speaking, you must know how to interpret and use new vocabulary words, and also understand how these words relate to one another. Sometimes words have the same meaning. Sometimes words are complete opposites of each other. Understanding how the words you read, write, and speak with relate to each other will deepen your understanding of how language works. This lesson will cover (1) synonyms, (2) antonyms, and (3) analogies.

Synonyms

A **synonym** is a word that has the same meaning or close to the same meaning as another word. For example, if you look up the words *irritated* and *annoyed* in a dictionary, you will discover that they both mean "showing or feeling slight anger." Similarly, if you were to look up *blissful* and *joyful*, you will see that they both mean "extremely happy." The dictionary definition of a word is called its **denotation**. This is a word's literal or direct meaning.

When you understand that there are multiple words that have the same **denotation**, it will broaden your vocabulary.

It is also important to know that words with similar meanings have **nuances**, or subtle differences.

One way that words have nuances is in their **shades of meanings**. This means that although they have a similar definition, if you look closely, you will see that they have slight differences.

FOR EXAMPLE

If you quickly glance at the following words, you will see that they all have a similar meaning. However, if you look closely, you will see that their meanings have subtle differences. You can see their differences by looking at their various **levels** or **degrees**:

LEAST $\longrightarrow$ MOST

---

nibble	bite	eat	devour
upset	angry	furious	irate
wet	soggy	soaked	drenched
good	great	amazing	phenomenal

Another way that words have nuance are in their **connotations.** A word's connotation is its **positive** or **negative** association. This can be the case even when two words have the same **denotations**, or dictionary definitions.

For example, the words *aroma* and *stench* both have a similar dictionary definition or **denotation**: "a smell." However, their **connotations** are quite different. *Aroma* has a **positive connotation** because it describes a *pleasant* smell. But *stench* has a **negative connotation** because it describes an unpleasant smell.

> **FOR EXAMPLE**
> Look at the following words. Although they have the same denotation, their connotations are very different:

Denotation	Positive Connotation	Negative Connotation
CLIQUE and *CLUB* both mean "a group of people."	*CLUB* has a positive connotation because it describes a group of people coming together to accomplish something.	*CLIQUE* has a negative connotation because it describes a group of people who exclude others.
INTERESTED and *NOSY* both mean "showing curiosity."	*INTERESTED* has a positive connotation because it means having a genuine curiosity about someone or something.	*NOSY* has a negative connotation because it describes who tries to pry information out of someone else to gossip or judge.
EMPLOY and *EXPLOIT* both mean "to use someone."	*EMPLOY* has a positive connotation because it means to use someone for a job.	*EXPLOIT* has a negative connotation because it means to use someone for one's own advantage.

Seeing that synonymous words have different **shades of meaning** and **connotations** will allow you to more precisely interpret and understand the nuances of language.

Antonyms

An **antonym** is a word that means the opposite or close to the opposite of another word. Think of an antonym as the direct opposite of a **synonym**. For example, *caring* and *apathetic* are antonyms because *caring* means "displaying concern and kindness for others" whereas *apathetic* means "showing no interest or concern."

Antonyms can fall under three categories:

Graded Antonyms:	Word pairs whose meanings are opposite and lie on a spectrum or continuum; there are many other words that fall between the two words. If you look at *hot* and *cold*, there are other words on this spectrum: *scalding,* **hot**, *warm, tepid, cool,* **cold**
Relational Antonyms:	Word pairs whose opposites make sense only in the context of the relationship between the two meanings. These two words could not exist without the other: ***open - close***
Complementary Antonyms:	Word pairs that have no degree of meaning at all; there are only two possibilities, one or the other: ***dead - alive***

CHAPTER 5 NUMBER AND QUANTITY

BASIC ADDITION AND SUBTRACTION

This lesson introduces the concept of numbers and their symbolic and graphical representations. It also describes how to add and subtract whole numbers.

Numbers

A **number** is a way to quantify a set of entities that share some characteristic. For example, a fruit basket might contain nine pieces of fruit. More specifically, it might contain three apples, two oranges, and four bananas. Note that a number is a quantity, but a **numeral** is the symbol that represents the number: 8 means the number eight, for instance.

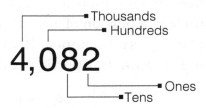

Although number representations vary, the most common is **base 10.** In base-10 format, each **digit** (or individual numeral) in a number is a quantity based on a multiple of 10. The base-10 system designates 0 through 9 as the numerals for zero through nine, respectively, and combines them to represent larger numbers. Thus, after counting from 1 to 9, the next number uses an additional digit: 10. That number means 1 group of 10 ones plus 0 additional ones. After 99, another digit is necessary, this time representing a hundred (10 sets of 10). This process of adding digits can go on indefinitely to express increasingly large numbers. For whole numbers, the rightmost digit is the ones place, the next digit to its left is the tens place, the next is the hundreds place, then the thousands place, and so on.

Classifying numbers can be convenient. The chart below lists a few common number sets.

Sets of Numbers	Members	Remarks
Natural numbers	1, 2, 3, 4, 5,...	The "counting" numbers
Whole numbers	0, 1, 2, 3, 4,...	The natural numbers plus 0
Integers	..., −3, −2, −1, 0, 1, 2, 3,...	The whole numbers plus all negative whole numbers
Real numbers	All numbers	The integers plus all fraction/decimal numbers in between
Rational numbers	All real numbers that can be expressed as p/q, where p and q are integers and q is nonzero	The natural numbers, whole numbers, and integers are all rational numbers
Irrational numbers	All real numbers that are not rational	The rational and irrational numbers together constitute the entire set of real numbers

Example

Jane has 4 pennies, 3 dimes, and 7 dollars. How many cents does she have?

   A. 347   B. 437   C. 734   D. 743

The correct answer is **C**. The correct solution is 734. A penny is 1 cent. A dime (10 pennies) is 10 cents, and a dollar (100 pennies) is 100 cents. Place the digits in base-10 format: 7 hundreds, 3 tens, 4 ones, or 734.

The Number Line

The **number line** is a model that illustrates the relationships among numbers. The complete number line is infinite and includes every real number—both positive and negative. A ruler, for example, is a portion of a number line that assigns a **unit** (such as inches or centimeters) to each number. Typically, number lines depict smaller numbers to the left and larger numbers to the right. For example, a portion of the number line centered on 0 might look like the following:

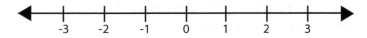

Because people learn about numbers in part through counting, they have a basic sense of how to order them. The number line builds on this sense by placing all the numbers (at least conceptually) from least to greatest. Whether a particular number is greater than or less than another is determined by comparing their relative positions. One number is greater than another if it is farther right on the number line. Likewise, a number is less than another if it is farther left on the number line. Symbolically, < means "is less than" and > means "is greater than." For example, $5 > 1$ and $9 < 25$.

Example

Place the following numbers in order from greatest to least: 5, –12, 0.

   A. 0, 5, –12   C. 5, 0, –12

   B. –12, 5, 0   D. –12, 0, 5

> **BE CAREFUL!**
>
> When ordering negative numbers, think of the number line. Although –10 > –2 may seem correct, it is incorrect. Because –10 is to the left of –2 on the number line, –10 < –2.

The correct answer is **C**. The correct solution is 5, 0, –12. Use the number line to order the numbers. Note that the question says *from greatest to least*.

Addition

Addition is the process of combining two or more numbers. For example, one set has 4 members and another set has 5 members. To combine the sets and find out how many members are in the new set, add 4 and 5 to get the **sum**. Symbolically, the expression is $4 + 5$, where + is the **plus sign**. Pictorially, it might look like the following:

$$\underset{\circ\;\circ}{\circ\circ} \;\; + \;\; \underset{\circ\;\;\circ\;\;\circ}{\circ\;\;\circ} \;\; = \;\; \underset{\circ\;\circ\;\circ\;\circ\;\circ}{\circ\;\circ\;\circ\;\circ}$$

To get the sum, combine the two sets of circles and then count them. The result is 9.

> **KEY POINT**
> The order of the numbers is irrelevant when adding.

Another way to look at addition involves the number line. When adding 4 + 5, for example, start at 4 on the number line and take 5 steps to the right. The stopping point will be 9, which is the sum.

Counting little pictures or using the number line works for small numbers, but it becomes unwieldy for large ones—even numbers such as 24 and 37 would be difficult to add quickly and accurately. A simple algorithm enables much faster addition of large numbers. It works with two or more numbers.

> **STEP BY STEP**
> **Step 1.** Stack the numbers, vertically aligning the digits for each place.
> **Step 2.** Draw a plus sign (+) to the left of the bottom number and draw a horizontal line below the last number.
> **Step 3.** Add the digits in the ones place.
> **Step 4.** If the sum from Step 3 is less than 10, write it in the same column below the horizontal line. Otherwise, write the first (ones) digit below the line, then **carry** the second (tens) digit to the top of the next column.
> **Step 5.** Going from right to left, repeat Steps 3–4 for the other places.
> **Step 6.** If applicable, write the remaining carry digit as the leftmost digit in the sum.

Example

Evaluate the expression 154 + 98.

A. 250   B. 252   C. 352   D. 15,498

The correct answer is **B**. The correct solution is 252. Carefully follow the addition algorithm (see below). The process involves carrying a digit twice.

$$
\begin{array}{r} 154 \\ +\ 98 \\ \hline \end{array}
\;\rightarrow\;
\begin{array}{r} {}^{1} \\ 154 \\ +\ 98 \\ \hline 2 \end{array}
\;\rightarrow\;
\begin{array}{r} {}^{11} \\ 154 \\ +\ 98 \\ \hline 52 \end{array}
\;\rightarrow\;
\begin{array}{r} {}^{11} \\ 154 \\ +\ 98 \\ \hline 252 \end{array}
$$

Subtraction

Subtraction is the inverse (opposite) of addition. Instead of representing the sum of numbers, it represents the difference between them. For example, given a set containing 15 members, subtracting 3 of those members yields a **difference** of 12. Using the **minus sign**, the expression for this operation is 15 − 3 = 12. As with addition, two approaches are counting pictures and using the number line. The first case might involve drawing 15 circles and then crossing off 3 of them; the difference is the number of remaining circles (12). To use the number line, begin at 15 and move left 3 steps to reach 12.

Again, these approaches are unwieldy for large numbers, but the subtraction algorithm eases evaluation by hand. This algorithm is only practical for two numbers at a time.

STEP BY STEP

Step 1. Stack the numbers, vertically aligning the digits in each place. Put the number you are subtracting *from* on top.

Step 2. Draw a minus sign (−) to the left of the bottom number and draw a horizontal line below the stack of numbers.

Step 3. Start at the ones place. If the digit at the top is larger than the digit below it, write the difference under the line. Otherwise, **borrow** from the top digit in the next-higher place by crossing it off, subtracting 1 from it, and writing the difference above it. Then add 10 to the digit in the ones place and perform the subtraction as normal.

Step 4. Going from right to left, repeat Step 3 for the rest of the places. If borrowing was necessary, make sure to use the new digit in each place, not the original one.

When adding or subtracting with negative numbers, the following rules are helpful. Note that x and y are used as placeholders for any real number.

$x + (-y) = x - y$

$-x - y = -(x + y)$

$(-x) + (-y) = -(x + y)$

$x - y = -(y - x)$

BE CAREFUL!

When dealing with numbers that have units (such as weights, currencies, or volumes), addition and subtraction are only possible when the numbers have the same unit. If necessary, convert one or more of them to equivalent numbers with the same unit.

Example

Kevin has 120 minutes to complete an exam. If he has already used 43, how many minutes does he have left?

A. 43   B. 77   C. 87   D. 163

The correct answer is **B**. The correct solution is 77. The first step is to convert this problem to a math expression. The goal is to find the difference between how many minutes Kevin has for the exam and how many he has left after 43 minutes have elapsed. The expression would be 120 − 43. Carefully follow the subtraction algorithm (see below). The process will involve borrowing a digit twice.

$$
\begin{array}{c}
120 \\
-\ 43 \\
\hline
\end{array}
\longrightarrow
\begin{array}{c}
{\scriptstyle 1\,10} \\
1\cancel{2}0 \\
-\ 43 \\
\hline
7
\end{array}
\longrightarrow
\begin{array}{c}
{\scriptstyle 0\ 11\,10} \\
\cancel{1}\cancel{2}0 \\
-\ 43 \\
\hline
77
\end{array}
$$

Let's Review!

- Numbers are positive and negative quantities and often appear in base-10 format.
- The number line illustrates the ordering of numbers.
- Addition is the combination of numbers. It can be performed by counting objects or pictures, moving on the number line, or using the addition algorithm.
- Subtraction is finding the difference between numbers. Like addition, it can be performed by counting, moving on the number line, or using the subtraction algorithm.

The correct answer is **A**. One approach is to find the prime factorization of 84. The factor tree shows that 84 = 2 × 2 × 3 × 7. Alternatively, note that answer D includes 1, which is not prime. Answer B includes 4, which is a composite number. Since answer C includes 5, which is not a factor of 84, the only possible answer is A.

Let's Review!

- A whole number is divisible by all of its factors, which are also whole numbers by definition.
- Multiples of a number are all possible products of that number and the integers.
- A prime number is a whole number greater than 1 that has no factors other than itself and 1.
- A composite number is a whole number greater than 1 that is not prime (that is, it has factors other than itself and 1).
- Even numbers are divisible by 2; odd numbers are not.
- Prime factorization yields all the prime factors of a number. The factor-tree method is one way to determine prime factorization.

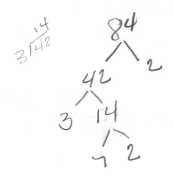

STANDARDS OF MEASURE

This lesson discusses the conversion within and between the standard system and the metric system and between 12-hour clock time and military time.

Length Conversions

The basic units of measure of length in the standard measurement system are inches, feet, yards, and miles. There are 12 inches (in.) in 1 foot (ft.), 3 feet (ft.) in 1 yard (yd.), and 5,280 feet (ft.) in 1 mile (mi.).

The basic unit of measure of metric length is meters. There are 1,000 millimeters (mm), 100, centimeters (cm), and 10 decimeters (dm) in 1 meter (m). There are 10 meters (m) in 1 dekameter (dam), 100 meters (m) in 1 hectometer (hm), and 1,000 meters (m) in 1 kilometer (km).

BE CAREFUL!

There are some cases where multiple conversions must be performed to determine the correct units.

To convert from one unit to the other, multiply by the appropriate factor.

Examples

1. **Convert 27 inches to feet.**

   A. 2 feet   B. 2.25 feet   C. 3 feet   D. 3.25 feet

   The correct answer is **B**. The correct solution is 2.25 feet. $27 \text{ in} \times \frac{1 \text{ ft}}{12 \text{ in}} = \frac{27}{12} = 2.25$ ft.

2. **Convert 67 millimeters to centimeters.**

   A. 0.0067 centimeters   C. 0.67 centimeters

   B. 0.067 centimeters   D. 6.7 centimeters

   The correct answer is **D**. The correct solution is 6.7 centimeters. $67 \text{ mm} \times \frac{1 \text{ cm}}{10 \text{ mm}} = \frac{67}{10} = 6.7$ cm.

Volume and Weight Conversions

There are volume conversion factors for standard and metric volumes.

The volume conversions for standard volume are shown in the table.

Measurement	Conversion
Pints (pt.) and fluid ounces (fl. oz.)	1 pint equals 16 fluid ounces
Quarts (qt.) and pints (pt.)	1 quart equals 2 pints
Quarts (qt.) and gallons (gal.)	1 gallon equals 4 quarts

The basic unit of volume for the metric system is liters. There are 1,000 milliliters (mL) in 1 liter (L) and 1,000 liters (L) in 1 kiloliter (kL).

There are weight conversion factors for standard and metric weights.

The basic unit of weight for the standard measurement system is pounds. There are

16 ounces (oz.) in 1 pound (lb.) and

2,000 pounds (lb.) in 1 ton (T).

The basic unit of weight for the metric system is grams.

KEEP IN MIND

The conversions within the metric system are multiples of 10.

Measurement	Conversion
Milligrams (mg) and grams (g)	1,000 milligrams equals 1 gram
Centigrams (cg) and grams (g)	100 centigrams equals 1 gram
Kilograms (kg) and grams (g)	1 kilogram equals 1,000 grams
Metric tons (t) and kilograms (kg)	1 metric ton equals 1,000 kilograms

Examples

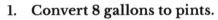

1. **Convert 8 gallons to pints.**

    A. 1 pint   B. 4 pints   C. 16 pints   D. 64 pints

    The correct answer is **D.** The correct solution is 64 pints. $8 \text{ gal} \times \frac{4 \text{ qt}}{1 \text{ gal}} \times \frac{2 \text{ pt}}{1 \text{ qt}} = 64 \text{ pt}$.

2. **Convert 7.5 liters to milliliters.**

    A. 75 milliliters   B. 750 milliliters   C. 7,500 milliliters   D. 75,000 milliliters

    The correct answer is **C.** The correct solution is 7,500 milliliters. $7.5 \text{ L} \times \frac{1,000 \text{ mL}}{1 \text{ L}} = 7,500 \text{ mL}$.

3. **Convert 12.5 pounds to ounces.**

    A. 142 ounces   B. 150 ounces   C. 192 ounces   D. 200 ounces

    The correct answer is **D.** The correct solution is 200 ounces. $12.5 \text{ lb} \times \frac{16 \text{ oz}}{1 \text{ lb}} = 200 \text{ oz}$.

4. **Convert 84 grams to centigrams.**

    A. 0.84 centigrams   B. 8.4 centigrams   C. 840 centigrams   D. 8,400 centigrams

    The correct answer is **D.** The correct solution is 8,400 centigrams. $84 \text{ g} \times \frac{100 \text{ cg}}{1 \text{ g}} = 8,400 \text{ cg}$.

Conversions between Standard and Metric Systems

The table shows the common conversions of length, volume, and weight between the standard and metric systems.

Measurement	Conversion
Centimeters (cm) and inches (in.)	2.54 centimeters equals 1 inch
Meters (m) and feet (ft.)	1 meter equals 3.28 feet
Kilometers (km) and miles (mi.)	1.61 kilometers equals 1 mile
Quarts (qt.) and liters (L)	1.06 quarts equals 1 liter
Liters (L) and gallons (gal.)	3.79 liters equals 1 gallon
Grams (g) and ounces (oz.)	28.3 grams equals 1 ounce
Kilograms (kg) and pounds (lb.)	1 kilogram equals 2.2 pounds

There are many additional conversion factors, but this lesson uses only the common ones. Most factors have been rounded to the nearest hundredth for accuracy.

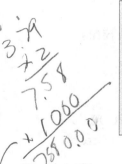

STEP BY STEP

Step 1. Choose the appropriate conversion factor within each system, if necessary.

Step 2. Choose the appropriate conversion factor from the standard and metric conversion.

Step 3. Multiply and simplify to the nearest hundredth.

Examples

1. **Convert 12 inches to centimeters.**

   A. 4.72 centimeters
   B. 14.54 centimeters
   C. 28.36 centimeters
   D. 30.48 centimeters

   The correct answer is **D**. The correct solution is 30.48 centimeters. $12 \text{ in} \times \frac{2.54 \text{ cm}}{1 \text{ in}} = 30.48 \text{ cm}$.

2. **Convert 8 kilometers to feet.**

   A. 13,118.01 feet
   B. 26,236.02 feet
   C. 34,003.20 feet
   D. 68,006.40 feet

   The correct answer is **B**. The correct solution is 26,236.02 feet. $8 \text{ km} \times \frac{1 \text{ mi}}{1.61 \text{ km}} \times \frac{5,280 \text{ ft}}{1 \text{ mi}} = \frac{42,240}{1.61} = 26{,}236.02 \text{ ft}$.

3. **Convert 2 gallons to milliliters.**

   A. 527 milliliters
   B. 758 milliliters
   C. 5,270 milliliters
   D. 7,580 milliliters

   The correct answer is **D**. The correct solution is 7,580 milliliters.
   $2 \text{ gal} \times \frac{3.79 \text{ L}}{1 \text{ gal}} \times \frac{1,000 \text{ mL}}{1 \text{ L}} = 7{,}580 \text{ mL}$.

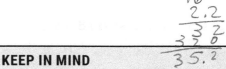

4. **Convert 16 kilograms to pounds.**

    A. 7.27 pounds   B. 18.2 pounds   C. 19.27 pounds   D. 35.2 pounds

The correct answer is **D**. The correct solution is 35.2 pounds. $16 \text{ kg} \times \frac{2.2 \text{ lb}}{1 \text{ kg}} = 35.2$ lb.

Time Conversions

Two ways to keep time are 12-hour clock time using a.m. and p.m. and military time based on a 24-hour clock. Keep these three key points in mind:

> **KEEP IN MIND**
> Midnight (12:00 a.m.) is 2400 or 0000 in military time.

- The hours from 1:00 a.m. to 12:59 p.m. are the same in both methods. For example, 9:15 a.m. in 12-hour clock time is 0915 in military time.
- From 1:00 p.m. to 11:59 p.m., add 12 hours to obtain military time. For example, 4:07 p.m. in 12-hour clock time is 1607 in military time.
- From 12:01 a.m. to 12:59 a.m. in 12-hour clock time, military time is from 0001 to 0059.

Example

Identify 9:27 p.m. in military time.

    A. 0927   B. 1927   C. 2127   D. 2427

The correct answer is **C**. The correct solution is 2127. Add 1200 to the time, 1200 + 927 = 2127.

Let's Review!

- To convert from one unit to another, choose the appropriate conversion factors.
- In many cases, it is necessary to use multiple conversion factors.

CHAPTER 5 NUMBER AND QUANTITY

PRACTICE QUIZ

1. Evaluate the expression 8 − 27.

   A. −35   C. 0

   B. −19   D. 19

2. Evaluate the expression 102 + 3 + 84 + 27.

   A. 105   C. 250

   B. 216   D. 513

3. How much change should a customer expect if she is buying a $53 item and hands the cashier two $50 bills?

   A. $3   C. $57

   B. $47   D. $100

4. When dealing with a series of multiplication and division operations, which is the correct approach to evaluating them?

   A. Evaluate all division operations first.

   B. Evaluate the expression from left to right.

   C. Evaluate all multiplication operations first.

   D. None of the above.

5. Evaluate the expression 28 × 43.

   A. 71   C. 1,204

   B. 196   D. 1,960

6. Evaluate the expression 3 + 1 − 5 + 2 − 6.

   A. −9   C. 0

   B. −5   D. 17

7. Which number is a factor of 128?

   A. 3   C. 12

   B. 6   D. 16

8. How many prime factors does 42 have?

   A. 1   C. 3

   B. 2   D. 4

9. If a factor tree for a prime factorization has four leaves—3, 2, 5, and 7—what is the number being factored?

   A. 7   C. 210

   B. 5   D. Not enough information

10. Convert 16,000 ounces to tons.

    A. 0.5 ton   C. 1.5 tons

    B. 1 ton   D. 2 tons

11. Convert 99 meters to kilometers.

    A. 0.0099 kilometers

    B. 0.099 kilometers

    C. 0.9 centimeters

    D. 9.9 centimeters

12. Identify 12:45 a.m. in military time.

    A. 0045   C. 1245

    B. 0145   D. 1345

CHAPTER 5 NUMBER AND QUANTITY PRACTICE QUIZ – ANSWER KEY

1. B. The correct solution is –19. Because the subtraction algorithm does not apply directly in this case (the first number is smaller than the second), first use the rule that $x - y = -(y - x)$. So, $8 - 27 = -(27 - 8)$. Applying the algorithm to $27 - 8$ yields 19, then $-(27 - 8) = -19$. **See Lesson: Basic Addition and Subtraction.**

2. B. The correct solution is 216. Use the addition algorithm. Add the numbers two at a time or all at once. The latter approach will involve two carry digits. **See Lesson: Basic Addition and Subtraction.**

3. B. The correct solution is $47. The customer gives the cashier $100, which is the sum of $50 and $50. To find out how much change she receives, calculate the difference between $100 and $53, which is $47. **See Lesson: Basic Addition and Subtraction.**

4. B. Multiplication and division have equivalent priority in the order of operations. In this case, the expression must be evaluated from left to right. **See Lesson: Basic Multiplication and Division.**

5. C. Use the multiplication algorithm. It involves adding 84 and 1,120 to get the product of 1,204. **See Lesson: Basic Multiplication and Division.**

6. B. This expression only involves addition and subtraction, but its evaluation must go from left to right. **See Lesson: Basic Multiplication and Division.**

$$3 + 1 - 5 + 2 - 6$$
$$4 - 5 + 2 - 6$$
$$(-1) + 2 - 6$$
$$1 - 6$$
$$-5$$

7. D. To determine whether a number is a factor of another number, divide the second number by the first number. If the quotient is whole, the first number is a factor. In this case, 128 is only divisible by 16. **See Lesson: Factors and Multiples.**

8. C. The prime factorization—for example, using a factor tree—shows that 42 has the prime factors 2, 3, and 7 because $2 \times 3 \times 7 = 42$. **See Lesson: Factors and Multiples.**

9. C. The number being factored in a prime factorization is the product of all its prime factors. The leaves in a factor tree are these prime factors. Therefore, the number is their product. In this case, it is $3 \times 2 \times 5 \times 7 = 210$. **See Lesson: Factors and Multiples.**

Two-Step Linear Equations

A two-step linear equation is in the form $ax + b = c$, where a is a non-zero constant and b and c are constants. There are two basic steps in solving this equation.

STEP BY STEP

Step 1. Use addition and subtraction properties of an equation to move the variable to one side of the equation and all number terms to the other side of the equation.

Step 2. Use multiplication and division properties of an equation to remove the value in front of the variable.

Examples

1. **Solve the equation for the unknown, $\frac{x}{-2} - 3 = 5$.**

   A. −16   B. −8   C. 8   D. 16

   The correct answer is **A**. The correct solution is −16.

$\frac{x}{-2} = 8$	Add 3 to both sides of the equation.
$x = -16$	Multiply both sides of the equation by −2.

2. **Solve the equation for the unknown, $4x + 3 = 8$.**

   A. −2   B. $-\frac{5}{4}$ C. $\frac{5}{4}$ D. 2

   The correct answer is **C**. The correct solution is $\frac{5}{4}$.

$4x = 5$	Subtract 3 from both sides of the equation.
$x = \frac{5}{4}$	Divide both sides of the equation by 4.

3. **Solve the equation for the unknown w, $P = 2l + 2w$.**

   A. $2P - 2l = w$ B. $\frac{P-2l}{2} = w$ C. $2P + 2l = w$ D. $\frac{P+2l}{2} = w$

   The correct answer is **B**. The correct solution is $\frac{P-2l}{2} = w$.

$P - 2l = 2w$	Subtract 2l from both sides of the equation.
$\frac{P-2l}{2} = w$	Divide both sides of the equation by 2.

Multi-Step Linear Equations

In these basic examples of linear equations, the solution may be evident, but these properties demonstrate how to use an opposite operation to solve for a variable. Using these properties, there are three steps in solving a complex linear equation.

> **STEP BY STEP**
> **Step 1.** Simplify each side of the equation. This includes removing parentheses, removing fractions, and adding like terms.
> **Step 2.** Use addition and subtraction properties of an equation to move the variable to one side of the equation and all number terms to the other side of the equation.
> **Step 3.** Use multiplication and division properties of an equation to remove the value in front of the variable.

In Step 2, all of the variables may be placed on the left side or the right side of the equation. The examples in this lesson will place all of the variables on the left side of the equation.

When solving for a variable, apply the same steps as above. In this case, the equation is not being solved for a value, but for a specific variable.

Examples

1. **Solve the equation for the unknown, $2(4x + 1)-5 = 3-(4x-3)$.**

   A. $\frac{1}{4}$ B. $\frac{3}{4}$ C. $\frac{4}{3}$ D. 4

   The correct answer is **B**. The correct solution is $\frac{3}{4}$.

$8x + 2-5 = 3-4x + 3$	Apply the distributive property.
$8x-3 = -4x + 6$	Combine like terms on both sides of the equation.
$12x-3 = 6$	Add $4x$ to both sides of the equation.
$12x = 9$	Add 3 to both sides of the equation.
$x = \frac{3}{4}$	Divide both sides of the equation by 12.

2. **Solve the equation for the unknown, $\frac{2}{3}x + 2 = -\frac{1}{2}x + 2(x + 1)$.**

   A. 0   B. 1   C. 2   D. 3

   The correct answer is **A**. The correct solution is 0.

$\frac{2}{3}x + 2 = -\frac{1}{2}x + 2x + 2$	Apply the distributive property.
$4x + 12 = -3x + 12x + 12$	Multiply all terms by the least common denominator of 6 to eliminate the fractions.
$4x + 12 = 9x + 12$	Combine like terms on the right side of the equation.
$-5x = 12$	Subtract $9x$ from both sides of the equation.
$-5x = 0$	Subtract 12 from both sides of the equation.
$x = 0$	Divide both sides of the equation by -5.

3. **Solve the equation for the unknown for** x, $y - y_1 = m(x - x_1)$.

A. $y - y_1 + m x_1$
B. $my - my_1 + m x_1$
C. $\frac{y - y_1 + x_1}{m}$
D. $\frac{y - y_1 + m x_1}{m}$

The correct answer is **D.** The correct solution is $\frac{y - y_1 + m x_1}{m}$

$y - y_1 = mx - m x_1$ Apply the distributive property.

$y - y_1 + m x_1 = mx$ Add $m x_1$ to both sides of the equation.

$\frac{y - y_1 + m x_1}{m} = x$ Divide both sides of the equation by m.

Solving Linear Inequalities

A **linear inequality** is similar to a linear equation, but it contains an inequality sign ($<$, $>$, $\leq$, $\geq$). Many of the steps for solving linear inequalities are the same as for solving linear equations. The major difference is that the solution is an infinite number of values. There are four properties to help solve a linear inequality.

Property	Definition	Example
Addition Property of Inequality	Add the same number to both sides of the inequality.	$x - 3 < 9$ $x - 3 + 3 < 9 + 3$ $x < 12$
Subtraction Property of Inequality	Subtract the same number from both sides of the inequality.	$x + 3 > 9$ $x + 3 - 3 > 9 - 3$ $x > 6$
Multiplication Property of Inequality (when multiplying by a positive number)	Multiply both sides of the inequality by the same number.	$\frac{x}{3} \geq 9$ $\frac{x}{3} \times 3 \geq 9 \times 3$ $x \geq 27$
Division Property of Inequality (when multiplying by a positive number)	Divide both sides of the inequality by the same number.	$3x \leq 9$ $\frac{3x}{3} \leq \frac{9}{3}$ $x \leq 3$
Multiplication Property of Inequality (when multiplying by a negative number)	Multiply both sides of the inequality by the same number.	$\frac{x}{-3} \geq 9$ $\frac{x}{-3} \times -3 \geq 9 \times -3$ $x \leq -27$
Division Property of Inequality (when multiplying by a negative number)	Divide both sides of the inequality by the same number.	$-3x \leq 9$ $\frac{-3x}{-3} \leq \frac{9}{-3}$ $x \geq -3$

Multiplying or dividing both sides of the inequality by a negative number reverses the sign of the inequality.

In these basic examples, the solution may be evident, but these properties demonstrate how to use an opposite operation to solve for a variable. Using these properties, there are three steps in solving a complex linear inequality.

> **STEP BY STEP**
>
> **Step 1.** Simplify each side of the inequality. This includes removing parentheses, removing fractions, and adding like terms.
>
> **Step 2.** Use addition and subtraction properties of an inequality to move the variable to one side of the equation and all number terms to the other side of the equation.
>
> **Step 3.** Use multiplication and division properties of an inequality to remove the value in front of the variable. Reverse the inequality sign if multiplying or dividing by a negative number.

In Step 2, all of the variables may be placed on the left side or the right side of the inequality. The examples in this lesson will place all of the variables on the left side of the inequality.

Examples

1. **Solve the inequality for the unknown, $3(2 + x) < 2(3x-1)$.**

    A. $x < -\frac{8}{3}$ 　　　　 B. $x > -\frac{8}{3}$ 　　　　 C. $x < \frac{8}{3}$ 　　　　 D. $x > \frac{8}{3}$

    The correct answer is **D**. The correct solution is $x > \frac{8}{3}$.

$6 + 3x < 6x-2$	Apply the distributive property.
$6-3x < -2$	Subtract $6x$ from both sides of the inequality.
$-3x < -8$	Subtract 6 from both sides of the inequality.
$x > \frac{8}{3}$	Divide both sides of the inequality by -3.

2. **Solve the inequality for the unknown, $\frac{1}{2}(2x-3) \geq \frac{1}{4}(2x + 1)-2$.**

    A. $x > -7$ 　　　　 B. $x > -3$ 　　　　 C. $x \geq -\frac{3}{2}$ 　　　　 D. $x \geq -\frac{1}{2}$

    The correct answer is **D**. The correct solution is $x \geq -\frac{1}{2}$.

$2(2x-3) \geq 2x + 1-8$	Multiply all terms by the least common denominator of 4 to eliminate the fractions.
$4x-6 \geq 2x + 1-8$	Apply the distributive property.
$4x-6 \geq 2x-7$	Combine like terms on the right side of the inequality.
$2x-6 \geq -7$	Subtract $2x$ from both sides of the inequality.
$2x \geq -1$	Add 6 to both sides of the inequality.
$x \geq -\frac{1}{2}$	Divide both sides of the inequality by 2.

Let's Review!

- A linear equation is an equation with one solution. Using opposite operations solves a linear equation.
- The process to solve a linear equation or inequality is to eliminate fractions and parentheses and combine like terms on the same side of the sign. Then, solve the equation or inequality by using inverse operations.

EQUATIONS WITH TWO VARIABLES

This lesson discusses solving a system of linear equations by substitution, elimination, and graphing, as well as solving a simple system of a linear and a quadratic equation.

Solving a System of Equations by Substitution

A **system of linear equations** is a set of two or more linear equations in the same variables. A solution to the system is an ordered pair that is a solution in all the equations in the system. The ordered pair (1, -2) is a solution for the system of equations $\begin{array}{l} 2x + y = 0 \\ -x + 2y = -5 \end{array}$ because $\begin{array}{l} 2(1) + (-2) = 0 \\ -1 + 2(-2) = -5 \end{array}$ makes both equations true.

One way to solve a system of linear equations is by substitution.

> **STEP BY STEP**
> **Step 1.** Solve one equation for one of the variables.
> **Step 2.** Substitute the expression from Step 1 into the other equation and solve for the other variable.
> **Step 3.** Substitute the value from Step 2 into one of the original equations and solve.

All systems of equations can be solved by substitution for any one of the four variables in the problem. The most efficient way of solving is locating the $1x$ or $1y$ in the equations because this eliminates the possibility of having fractions in the equations.

Examples

1. **Solve the system of equations,** $\begin{array}{l} x = y + 6 \\ 4x + 5y = 60 \end{array}$.

   A. (10, 12) B. (6, 12) C. (6, 4) D. (10, 4)

   The correct answer is **D.** The correct solution is (10, 4).

   The first equation is already solved for x.

$4(y + 6) + 5y = 60$	Substitute $y + 6$ in for x in the first equation.
$4y + 24 + 5y = 60$	Apply the distributive property.
$9y + 24 = 60$	Combine like terms on the left side of the equation.
$9y = 36$	Subtract 24 from both sides of the equation.
$y = 4$	Divide both sides of the equation by 9.
$x = 4 + 6$	Substitute 4 in the first equation for y.
$x = 10$	Simplify using order of operations.

2. **Solve the system of equations,** $\begin{array}{c} 3x + 2y = 41 \\ -4x + y = -18 \end{array}$.

A. (5, 13) B. (6, 6) C. (7, 10) D. (10, 7)

The correct answer is **C**. The correct solution is (7, 10).

$y = 4x{-}18$	Solve the second equation for y by adding $4x$ to both sides of the equation.
$3x + 2(4x{-}18) = 41$	Substitute $4x{-}18$ in for y in the first equation.
$3x + 8x{-}36 = 41$	Apply the distributive property.
$11x{-}36 = 41$	Combine like terms on the left side of the equation.
$11x = 77$	Add 36 to both sides of the equation.
$x = 7$	Divide both sides of the equation by 11.
$-4(7) + y = -18$	Substitute 7 in the second equation for x.
$-28 + y = -18$	Simplify using order of operations.
$y = 10$	Add 28 to both sides of the equation.

Solving a System of Equations by Elimination

Another way to solve a system of linear equations is by elimination.

STEP BY STEP

Step 1. Multiply, if necessary, one or both equations by a constant so at least one pair of like terms has opposite coefficients.

Step 2. Add the equations to eliminate one of the variables.

Step 3. Solve the resulting equation.

Step 4. Substitute the value from Step 3 into one of the original equations and solve for the other variable.

All system of equations can be solved by the elimination method for any one of the four variables in the problem. One way of solving is locating the variables with opposite coefficients and adding the equations. Another approach is multiplying one equation to obtain opposite coefficients for the variables.

Examples

1. Solve the system of equations, $\begin{aligned} 3x + 5y &= 28 \\ -4x - 5y &= -34 \end{aligned}$.

    A. (12, 6)   B. (6, 12)   C. (6, 2)   D. (2, 6)

    The correct answer is **C.** The correct solution is (6, 2).

$-x = -6$	Add the equations.
$x = 6$	Divide both sides of the equation by -1.
$3(6) + 5y = 28$	Substitute 6 in the first equation for x.
$18 + 5y = 28$	Simplify using order of operations.
$5y = 10$	Subtract 18 from both sides of the equation.
$y = 2$	Divide both sides of the equation by 5.

2. Solve the system of equations, $\begin{aligned} -5x + 5y &= 0 \\ 2x - 3y &= -3 \end{aligned}$.

    A. (2, 2)   B. (3, 3)   C. (6, 6)   D. (9, 9)

    The correct answer is **B.** The correct solution is (3, 3).

$-10x + 10y = 0$	Multiply all terms in the first equation by 2.
$10x - 15y = -15$	Multiply all terms in the second equation by 5.
$-5y = -15$	Add the equations.
$y = 3$	Divide both sides of the equation by -5.
$2x - 3(3) = -3$	Substitute 3 in the second equation for y.
$2x - 9 = -3$	Simplify using order of operations.
$2x = 6$	Add 9 to both sides of the equation.
$x = 3$	Divide both sides of the equation by 2.

Solving a System of Equations by Graphing

Graphing is a third method of a solving system of equations. The point of intersection is the solution for the graph. This method is a great way to visualize each graph on a coordinate plane.

STEP BY STEP

Step 1. Graph each equation in the coordinate plane.

Step 2. Estimate the point of intersection.

Step 3. Check the point by substituting for x and y in each equation of the original system.

The best approach to graphing is to obtain each line in slope-intercept form. Then, graph the y-intercept and use the slope to find additional points on the line.

Example

Solve the system of equations by graphing, $\begin{array}{l} y = 3x-2 \\ y = x-4 \end{array}$.

A.

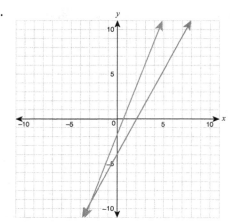

C.

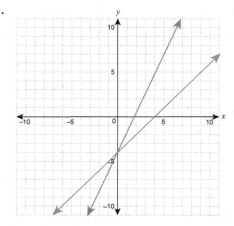

B.

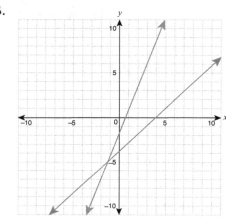

D.

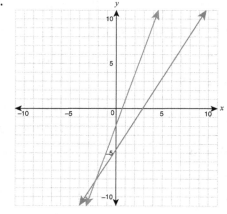

The correct answer is **B**. The correct graph has the two lines intersect at (-1, -5).

Solving a System of a Linear Equation and an Equation of a Circle

There are many other types of systems of equations. One example is the equation of a line $y = mx$ and the equation of a circle $x^2 + y^2 = r^2$ where r is the radius. With this system of equations, there can be two ordered pairs that intersect between the line and the circle. If there is one ordered pair, the line is tangent to the circle.

This system of equations is solved by substituting the expression mx in for y in the equation of a circle. Then, solve the equation for x. The values for x are substituted into the linear equation to find the value for y.

KEEP IN MIND

There will be two solutions in many cases with the system of a linear equation and an equation of a circle.

Example

Solve the system of equations, $\begin{matrix} y = -3x \\ x^2 + y^2 = 10 \end{matrix}$.

A. $(1, 3)$ and $(-1, -3)$ C. $(-3, 10)$ and $(3, -10)$

B. $(1, -3)$ and $(-1, 3)$ D. $(3, 10)$ and $(-3, -10)$

The correct answer is **B.** The correct solutions are $(1, -3)$ and $(-1, 3)$.

$x^2 + (-3x)^2 = 10$	Substitute $-3x$ in for y in the second equation.
$x^2 + 9x^2 = 10$	Apply the exponent.
$10x^2 = 10$	Combine like terms on the left side of the equation.
$x^2 = 1$	Divide both sides of the equation by 10.
$x = \pm 1$	Apply the square root to both sides of the equation.
$y = -3(1) = -3$	Substitute 1 in the first equation and multiply.
$y = -3(-1) = 3$	Substitute -1 in the first equation and multiply.

Let's Review!

- There are three ways to solve a system of equations: graphing, substitution, and elimination. Using any method will result in the same solution for the system of equations.
- Solving a system of a linear equation and an equation of a circle uses substitution and usually results in two solutions.

SOLVING REAL-WORLD MATHEMATICAL PROBLEMS

This lesson introduces solving real-world mathematical problems by using estimation and mental computation. This lesson also includes real-world applications involving integers, fractions, and decimals.

Estimating

Estimations are rough calculations of a solution to a problem. The most common use for estimation is completing calculations without a calculator or other tool. There are many estimation techniques, but this lesson focuses on integers, decimals, and fractions.

> **KEEP IN MIND**
> An estimation is an educated guess at the solution to a problem.

To round a whole number, round the value to the nearest ten or hundred. The number 142 rounds to 140 for the nearest ten and to 100 for the nearest hundred. The context of the problem determines the place value to which to round.

In most problems with fractions and decimals, the context of the problem requires rounding to the nearest whole number. Rounding these values makes calculation easier and provides an accurate estimation to the solution of the problem.

Other estimation strategies include the following:

- Using friendly or compatible numbers
- Using numbers that are easy to compute
- Adjusting numbers after rounding

Example

There are 168 hours in a week. Carson does the following:

- Sleeps 7.5 hours each day of the week
- Goes to school 6.75 hours five days a week
- Practices martial arts and basketball 1.5 hours each three times a week
- Reads and studies 1.75 hours every day
- Eats 1.5 hours every day

Estimate the remaining number of hours.

A. 20   B. 30   C. 40   D. 50

The correct answer is **C**. The correct solution is 40. He sleeps about 56 hours, goes to school for 35 hours, practices for 12 hours, reads and studies for about 14 hours, and eats for about 14 hours. This is 131 hours. Therefore, Carson has about 40 hours remaining.

Real-World Integer Problems

The following five steps can make solving word problems easier:

1. Read the problem for understanding.
2. Visualize the problem by drawing a picture or diagram.
3. Make a plan by writing an expression to represent the problem.
4. Solve the problem by applying mathematical techniques.
5. Check the answer to make sure it answers the question asked.

BE CAREFUL!
Make sure that you read the problem fully before visualizing and making a plan.

In basic problems, the solution may be evident, but make sure to demonstrate knowledge of writing the expression. In multi-step problems, first make a plan with the correct expression. Then, apply the correct calculation.

Examples

1. **The temperature on Monday was –9°F, and on Tuesday it was 8°F. What is the difference in temperature, in °F?**

   A. –17°   B. –1°   C. 1°   D. 17°

   The correct answer is **D**. The correct solution is 17° because 8–(–9) = 17°F.

2. **A golfer's last 12 rounds were –2, +4, –3, –1, +5, +3, –4, –5, –2, –6, –1, and 0. What is the average of these rounds?**

   A. –12   B. –1   C. 1   D. 12

   The correct answer is **B**. The correct solution is –1. The total of the scores is –12. The average is –12 divided by 12, which is –1.

Real-World Fraction and Decimal Problems

The five steps in the previous section are applicable to solving real-world fraction and decimal problems. The expressions with one step require only one calculation: addition, subtraction, multiplication, or division. The problems with multiple steps require writing out the expressions and performing the correct calculations.

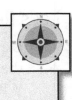

KEEP IN MIND
Estimating the solution first can help determine if a calculation is completed correctly.

Examples

1. The length of a room is $7\frac{2}{3}$ feet. When the length of the room is doubled, what is the new length in feet?

   A. $14\frac{2}{3}$ B. $15\frac{1}{3}$ C. $15\frac{2}{3}$ D. $16\frac{1}{3}$

   The correct answer is **B**. The correct solution is $15\frac{1}{3}$. The length is multiplied by 2, $7\frac{2}{3} \times 2 = \frac{23}{3} \times \frac{2}{1} = \frac{46}{3} = 15\frac{1}{3}$ feet.

2. A fruit salad is a mixture of $1\frac{3}{4}$ pounds of apples, $2\frac{1}{4}$ pounds of grapes, and $1\frac{1}{4}$ pounds of bananas. After the fruit is mixed, $1\frac{1}{2}$ pounds are set aside, and the rest is divided into three containers. What is the weight in pounds of one container?

   A. $1\frac{1}{5}$ B. $1\frac{1}{4}$ C. $1\frac{1}{3}$ D. $1\frac{1}{2}$

   The correct answer is **B**. The correct solution is $1\frac{1}{4}$. The amount available for the containers is $1\frac{3}{4} + 2\frac{1}{4} + 1\frac{1}{4} - 1\frac{1}{2} = 5\frac{1}{4} - 1\frac{1}{2} = 5\frac{1}{4} - 1\frac{2}{4} = 4\frac{5}{4} - 1\frac{2}{4} = 3\frac{3}{4}$. This amount is divided into three containers, $3\frac{3}{4} \div 3 = \frac{15}{4} \times \frac{15}{12} = 1\frac{3}{12} = 1\frac{1}{4}$ pounds.

3. In 2016, a town had 17.4 inches of snowfall. In 2017, it had 45.2 inches of snowfall. What is the difference in inches?

   A. 27.2   B. 27.8   C. 28.2   D. 28.8

   The correct answer is **B**. The correct solution is 27.8 because $45.2 - 17.4 = 27.8$ inches.

4. Mike bought items that cost $4.78, $3.49, $6.79, $9.78, and $14.05. He had a coupon worth $5.00. If he paid with a $50.00 bill, then how much change does he receive?

   A. $16.11   B. $18.11   C. $21.11   D. $23.11

   The correct answer is **A**. The correct solution is $16.11. The total bill is $38.89, less the coupon is $33.89. The amount of change is $50.00 - $33.89 = $16.11.

Let's Review!

- Using estimation is beneficial to determine an approximate solution to the problem when the numbers are complex.
- When solving a word problem with integers, fractions, or decimals, first read and visualize the problem. Then, make a plan, solve, and check the answer.

CHAPTER 6 ALGEBRA PRACTICE QUIZ

1. Which decimal is the greatest?

   A. 1.7805

   C. 1.7085

   B. 1.5807

   D. 1.8057

2. Change $0.\overline{63}$ to a fraction. Simplify completely.

   A. $\frac{5}{9}$

   C. $\frac{2}{3}$

   B. $\frac{7}{11}$

   D. $\frac{5}{6}$

3. Write $0.\overline{1}$ as a percent.

   A. $0.\overline{1}\%$

   C. $11.\overline{1}\%$

   B. $1.\overline{1}\%$

   D. $111.\overline{1}\%$

4. Solve the equation for the unknown, $4x + 3 = 8$.

   A. -2

   C. $\frac{5}{4}$

   B. $-\frac{5}{4}$

   D. 2

5. Solve the inequality for the unknown, $3x + 5-2(x + 3) > 4(1-x) + 5$.

   A. $x > 2$

   C. $x > 10$

   B. $x > 9$

   D. $x > 17$

6. Solve the equation for h, $SA = 2\pi rh + 2\pi r^2$.

   A. $2\pi rSA-2\pi r^2 = h$

   B. $2\pi rSA + 2\pi r^2 = h$

   C. $\frac{SA-2\pi r^2}{2\pi r} = h$

   D. $\frac{SA + 2\pi r^2}{2\pi r} = h$

7. Solve the system of equations, $y = -2x + 3$ $y + x = 5$.

   A. $(-2, 7)$

   C. $(2, -7)$

   B. $(-2, -7)$

   D. $(2, 7)$

8. Solve the system of equations, $2x-3y = -1$ $x + 2y = 24$.

   A. $(7, 10)$

   C. $(6, 8)$

   B. $(10, 7)$

   D. $(8, 6)$

9. Divide $1\frac{5}{6} \div 1\frac{1}{3}$.

   A. $1\frac{5}{18}$

   C. $2\frac{4}{9}$

   B. $1\frac{3}{8}$

   D. $3\frac{1}{6}$

10. Multiply $1\frac{1}{4} \times 1\frac{1}{2}$.

    A. $1\frac{1}{8}$

    C. $1\frac{2}{3}$

    B. $1\frac{1}{3}$

    D. $1\frac{7}{8}$

11. Divide $\frac{1}{10} \div \frac{2}{3}$.

    A. $\frac{1}{15}$

    C. $\frac{3}{20}$

    B. $\frac{1}{10}$

    D. $\frac{3}{5}$

12. A store has 75 pounds of bananas. Eight customers buy 3.3 pounds, five customers buy 4.25 pounds, and one customer buys 6.8 pounds. How many pounds are left in stock?

    A. 19.45

    C. 20.45

    B. 19.55

    D. 20.55

13. Solve the system of equations by graphing, $\begin{array}{l} 3x + y = -1 \\ 2x - y = -4 \end{array}$.

A.

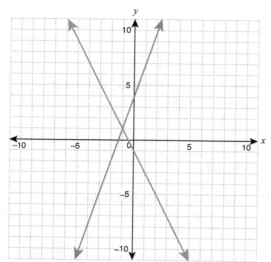

C.

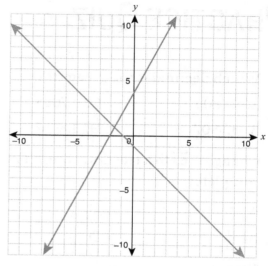

B.

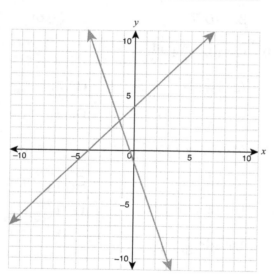

D.

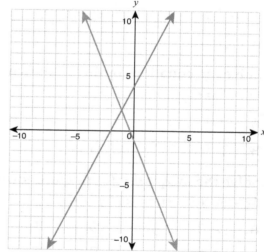

14. A rectangular garden needs a border. The length is $15\frac{3}{5}$ feet, and the width is $3\frac{2}{3}$ feet. What is the perimeter in feet?

   A. $18\frac{5}{8}$ C. $37\frac{1}{4}$

   B. $19\frac{4}{15}$ D. $38\frac{8}{15}$

15. A historical society has 8 tours daily 5 days a week, with 32 people on each tour. Estimate the number of people who can be on the tour in 50 weeks.

   A. 25,000   C. 75,000

   B. 50,000   D. 100,000

CHAPTER 6 ALGEBRA
PRACTICE QUIZ — ANSWER KEY

1. D. The correct solution is 1.8057 because 1.8057 contains the largest value in the tenths place. **See Lesson: Decimals and Fractions.**

2. B. The correct solution is $\frac{7}{11}$. Let $n = 0.\overline{63}$ and $100n = 63.\overline{63}$. Then, $100n - n = 63.\overline{63} - 0.\overline{63}$ resulting in $99n = 63$ and solution of $n = \frac{63}{99} = \frac{7}{11}$. **See Lesson: Decimals and Fractions.**

3. C. The correct answer is $11.\overline{1}\%$ because $0.\overline{1}$ as a percent is $0.\overline{1} \times 100 = 11.\overline{1}\%$. **See Lesson: Decimals and Fractions.**

4. C. The correct solution is $\frac{5}{4}$.

$4x = 5$	Subtract 3 from both sides of the equation.
$x = \frac{5}{4}$	Divide both sides of the equation by 4.

See Lesson: Equations with One Variable.

5. A. The correct solution is $x > 2$.

$3x + 5 - 2x - 6 > 4 - 4x + 5$	Apply the distributive property.
$x - 1 > -4x + 9$	Combine like terms on both sides of the inequality.
$5x - 1 > 9$	Add $4x$ to both sides of the inequality.
$5x > 10$	Add 1 to both sides of the inequality.
$x > 2$	Divide both sides of the inequality by 5.

See Lesson: Equations with One Variable.

6. C. The correct solution is $\frac{SA - 2\pi r^2}{2\pi r} = h$.

$SA - 2\pi r^2 = 2\pi rh$	Subtract $2\pi r^2$ from both sides of the equation.
$\frac{SA - 2\pi r^2}{2\pi r} = h$	Divide both sides of the equation by $2\pi r$.

See Lesson: Equations with One Variable.

7. A. The correct solution is (-2, 7).

	The first equation is already solved for y.
$-2x + 3 + x = 5$	Substitute $-2x + 3$ in for y in the second equation.
$-x + 3 = 5$	Combine like terms on the left side of the equation.
$-x = 2$	Subtract 3 from both sides of the equation.
$x = -2$	Divide both sides of the equation by -1.
$y = -2(-2) + 3$	Substitute -2 in the first equation for x.
$y = 4 + 3 = 7$	Simplify using order of operations.

See Lesson: Equations with Two Variables.

8. B. The correct solution is (10, 7).

$-2x - 4y = -48$	Multiply all terms in the second equation by -2.
$-7y = -49$	Add the equations.
$y = 7$	Divide both sides of the equation by -7.
$x + 2(7) = 24$	Substitute 7 in the second equation for y.
$x + 14 = 24$	Simplify using order of operations.
$x = 10$	Subtract 14 from both sides of the equation.

See Lesson: Equations with Two Variables.

9. B. The correct answer is $1\frac{3}{8}$ because $\frac{11}{6} \div \frac{4}{3} = \frac{11}{6} \times \frac{3}{4} = \frac{33}{24} = 1\frac{9}{24} = 1\frac{3}{8}$. **See Lesson: Multiplication and Division of Fractions.**

10. D. The correct solution is $1\frac{7}{8}$ because $\frac{5}{4} \times \frac{3}{2} = \frac{15}{8} = 1\frac{7}{8}$. **See Lesson: Multiplication and Division of Fractions.**

11. C. The correct solution is $\frac{3}{20}$ because $\frac{1}{10} \times \frac{3}{2} = \frac{3}{20}$. **See Lesson: Multiplication and Division of Fractions.**

12. D. The correct solution is 20.55 because the number of pounds purchased is $8(3.3) + 5(4.25) + 6.8 = 26.4 + 21.25 + 6.8 = 54.45$ pounds. The number of pounds remaining is $75 - 54.45 = 20.55$ pounds. **See Lesson: Solving Real-World Mathematical Problems.**

13. D. The correct graph has the two lines intersect at (-1, 2). **See Lesson: Equations with Two Variables.**

14. D. The correct solution is $38\frac{8}{15}$ because $15\frac{3}{5} + 3\frac{2}{3} = 15\frac{9}{15} + 3\frac{10}{15} = 18\frac{19}{15}(2) = \frac{289}{15} \times \frac{2}{1} = \frac{578}{15} = 38\frac{8}{15}$ feet. **See Lesson: Solving Real-World Mathematical Problems.**

15. C. The correct solution is 75,000 because by estimation $10(5)(30)(50) = 75,000$ people can be on the tour in 50 weeks. **See Lesson: Solving Real-World Mathematical Problems.**

CHAPTER 7 FUNCTIONS

SOLVING QUADRATIC EQUATIONS

This lesson introduces solving quadratic equations by the square root method, completing the square, factoring, and using the quadratic formula.

Solving Quadratic Equations by the Square Root Method

A **quadratic equation** is an equation where the highest variable is squared. The equation is in the form $ax^2 + bx + c = 0$, where a is a non-zero constant and b and c are constants. There are at most two solutions to the equation because the highest variable is squared. There are many methods to solve a quadratic equation.

This section will explore solving a quadratic equation by the square root method. The equation must be in the form of $ax^2 = c$, or there is no x term.

STEP BY STEP

Step 1. Use multiplication and division properties of an equation to remove the value in front of the variable.

Step 2. Apply the square root to both sides of the equation.

Note: The positive and negative square root make the solution true. For the equation $x^2 = 9$, the solutions are –3 and 3 because $3^2 = 9$ and $(-3)^2 = 9$.

Example

Solve the equation by the square root method, $4x^2 = 64$.

A. 4   B. 8   C. ±4   D. ±8

The correct answer is **C**. The correct solution is ±4.

$x^2 = 16$	Divide both sides of the equation by 4.
$x = \pm 4$	Apply the square root to both sides of the equation.

Solving Quadratic Equations by Completing the Square

A quadratic equation in the form $x^2 + bx$ can be solved by a process known as completing the square. The best time to solve by completing the square is when the b term is even.

> **STEP BY STEP**
> **Step 1.** Divide all terms by the coefficient of x^2.
> **Step 2.** Move the number term to the right side of the equation.
> **Step 3.** Complete the square $\left(\frac{b}{2}\right)^2$ and add this value to both sides of the equation.
> **Step 4.** Factor the left side of the equation.
> **Step 5.** Apply the square root to both sides of the equation.
> **Step 6.** Use addition and subtraction properties to move all number terms to the right side of the equation.

Examples

1. **Solve the equation by completing the square, $x^2 - 8x + 12 = 0$.**

   A. −2 and −6　　　　B. 2 and −6　　　　C. −2 and 6　　　　D. 2 and 6

   The correct answer is **D**. The correct solutions are 2 and 6.

$x^2 - 8x = -12$	Subtract 12 from both sides of the equation.
$x^2 - 8x + 16 = -12 + 16$	Complete the square, $\left(-\frac{8}{2}\right)^2 = (-4)^2 = 16$.
	Add 16 to both sides of the equation.
$x^2 - 8x + 16 = 4$	Simplify the right side of the equation.
$(x-4)^2 = 4$	Factor the left side of the equation.
$x - 4 = \pm 2$	Apply the square root to both sides of the equation.
$x = 4 \pm 2$	Add 4 to both sides of the equation.
$x = 4 - 2 = 2,\ x = 4 + 2 = 6$	Simplify the right side of the equation.

2. **Solve the equation by completing the square, $x^2 + 6x - 8 = 0$.**

   A. $-3 \pm \sqrt{17}$　　　　B. $3 \pm \sqrt{17}$　　　　C. $-3 \pm \sqrt{8}$　　　　D. $3 \pm \sqrt{8}$

   The correct answer is **A**. The correct solutions are $-3 \pm \sqrt{17}$.

$x^2 + 6x = 8$	Add 8 to both sides of the equation.
$x^2 + 6x + 9 = 8 + 9$	Complete the square, $\left(\frac{6}{2}\right)^2 = 3^2 = 9$. Add 9 to both sides of the equation.
$x^2 + 6x + 9 = 17$	Simplify the right side of the equation.
$(x + 3)^2 = 17$	Factor the left side of the equation.
$x + 3 = \pm \sqrt{17}$	Apply the square root to both sides of the equation.
$x = -3 \pm \sqrt{17}$	Subtract 3 from both sides of the equation.

Solving Quadratic Equations by Factoring

Factoring can only be used when a quadratic equation is factorable; other methods are needed to solve quadratic equations that are not factorable.

STEP BY STEP

Step 1. Simplify if needed by clearing any fractions and parentheses.

Step 2. Write the equation in standard form, $ax^2 + bx + c = 0$.

Step 3. Factor the quadratic equation.

Step 4. Set each factor equal to zero.

Step 5. Solve the linear equations using inverse operations.

The quadratic equation will have two solutions if the factors are different or one solution if the factors are the same.

Examples

1. **Solve the equation by factoring, $x^2 - 13x + 42 = 0$.**

   A. $-6, -7$ B. $-6, 7$ C. $6, -7$ D. $6, 7$

   The correct answer is **D**. The correct solutions are 6 and 7.

$(x-6)(x-7) = 0$	Factor the equation.
$(x-6) = 0$ or $(x-7) = 0$	Set each factor equal to 0.
$x-6 = 0$	Add 6 to both sides of the equation to solve for the first factor.
$x = 6$	
$x-7 = 0$	Add 7 to both sides of the equation to solve for the second factor.
$x = 7$	

2. **Solve the equation by factoring, $9x^2 + 30x + 25 = 0$.**

   A. $-\frac{5}{3}$ B. $-\frac{3}{5}$ C. $\frac{3}{5}$ D. $\frac{5}{3}$

   The correct answer is **A**. The correct solution is $-\frac{5}{3}$.

$(3x + 5)(3x + 5) = 0$	Factor the equation.
$(3x + 5) = 0$ or $(3x + 5) = 0$	Set each factor equal to 0.
$(3x + 5) = 0$	Set one factor equal to zero since both factors are the same.
$3x + 5 = 0$	Subtract 5 from both sides of the equation and divide both sides of the equation by 3 to solve.
$3x = -5$	
$x = -\frac{5}{3}$	

Solving Quadratic Equations by the Quadratic Formula

Many quadratic equations are not factorable. Another method of solving a quadratic equation is by using the quadratic formula. This method can be used to solve any quadratic equation in the form . Using the coefficients a, b, and c, the quadratic formula is $x = \frac{-b \pm \sqrt{b^2-4ac}}{2a}$. The values are substituted into the formula, and applying the order of operations finds the solution(s) to the equation.

The solution of the quadratic formula in these examples will be exact or estimated to three decimal places. There may be cases where the exact solutions to the quadratic formula are used.

KEEP IN MIND

Watch the negative sign in the formula. Remember that a number squared is always positive.

Examples

1. **Solve the equation by the quadratic formula, $x^2 - 5x - 6 = 0$.**

    A. –6 and –1   B. 6 and –1   C. –6 and 1   D. 6 and 1

    The correct answer is **B**. The correct solutions are 6 and –1.

$x = \frac{-(-5) \pm \sqrt{(-5)^2 - 4(1)(-6)}}{2(1)}$	Substitute 1 for a, –5 for b, and –6 for c.
$x = \frac{5 \pm \sqrt{25-(-24)}}{2}$	Apply the exponent and perform the multiplication.
$x = \frac{5 \pm \sqrt{49}}{2}$	Perform the subtraction.
$x = \frac{5 \pm 7}{2}$	Apply the square root.
$x = \frac{5+7}{2}, \; x = \frac{5-7}{2}$	Separate the problem into two expressions.
$x = \frac{12}{2} = 6, \; x = \frac{-2}{2} = -1$	Simplify the numerator and divide.

2. **Solve the equation by the quadratic formula, $2x^2 + 4x - 5 = 0$.**

    A. –0.87 and –2.87   B. 0.87 and –2.87   C. –0.87 and 2.87   D. 0.87 and 2.87

    The correct answer is **B**. The correct solutions are –0.87 and –2.87.

$x = \frac{-4 \pm \sqrt{4^2 - 4(2)(-5)}}{2(2)}$	Substitute 2 for a, 4 for b, and –5 for c.
$x = \frac{-4 \pm \sqrt{16-(-40)}}{4}$	Apply the exponent and perform the multiplication.
$x = \frac{-4 \pm \sqrt{56}}{4}$	Perform the subtraction.
$x = \frac{-4 \pm 7.48}{4}$	Apply the square root.
$x = \frac{-4 + 7.48}{4}, \; x = \frac{-4 - 7.48}{4}$	Separate the problem into two expressions.
$x = \frac{3.48}{4} = 0.87, \; x = \frac{-11.48}{4} = -2.87$	Simplify the numerator and divide.

Let's Review!

There are four methods to solve a quadratic equation algebraically:

- The square root method is used when there is a squared variable term and a constant term.
- Completing the square is used when there is a squared variable term and an even variable term.
- Factoring is used when the equation can be factored.
- The quadratic formula can be used for any quadratic equation.

Express Large or Small Quantities as Multiples of 10

Scientific notation is a large or small number written in two parts. The first part is a number between 1 and 10. In these problems, the first digit will be a single digit. The number is followed by a multiple to a power of 10. A positive integer exponent means the number is greater than 1, while a negative integer exponent means the number is smaller than 1.

> **KEEP IN MIND**
>
> A positive exponent in scientific notation represents a large number, while a negative exponent represents a small number.

The number 3×10^4 is the same as $3 \times 10,000 = 30,000$.

The number 3×10^{-4} is the same as $3 \times 0.0001 = 0.0003$.

For example, the population of the United States is about 3×10^8, and the population of the world is about 7×10^9. The population of the United States is 300,000,000, and the population of the world is 7,000,000,000. The world population is about 20 times larger than the population of the United States.

Examples

1. **The population of China is about 1×10^9, and the population of the United States is about 3×10^8. How many times larger is the population of China than the population of the United States?**

   A. 2   B. 3   C. 4   D. 5

   The correct answer is **B**. The correct solution is 3 because the population of China is about 1,000,000,000 and the population of the United States is about 300,000,000. So the population is about 3 times larger.

2. **A red blood cell has a length of 8×10^{-6} meter, and a skin cell has a length of 3×10^{-5} meter. How many times larger is the skin cell?**

   A. 1   B. 2   C. 3   D. 4

   The correct answer is **D**. The correct solution is 4 because 3×10^{-5} is 0.00003 and 8×10^{-6} is 0.000008. So, the skin cell is about 4 times larger.

Let's Review!

- The properties and rules of exponents are applicable to generate equivalent expressions.
- Only a few whole numbers out of the set of whole numbers are perfect squares. Perfect cubes can be positive or negative.
- Numbers expressed in scientific notation are useful to compare large or small numbers.

CHAPTER 7 FUNCTIONS
PRACTICE QUIZ

1. Multiply, $(x-1)(x^2 + 2x + 3)$.

   A. $x^3 + x^2 + x - 3$ C. $x^3 + x^2 - x - 3$

   B. $x^3 - x^2 - x - 3$ D. $x^3 - x^2 + x - 3$

2. Apply the polynomial identity to rewrite $9x^2 - 30x + 25$.

   A. $(3x + 5)(3x - 5)$ C. $(3x - 5)(3x - 1)$

   B. $(3x - 5)^2$ D. $(3x - 5)(3x + 1)$

3. Perform the operation, $(3y^2 + 4y) - (5y^3 - 2y^2 + 3)$.

   A. $-5y^3 + y^2 + 4y - 3$

   B. $-5y^3 + 5y^2 + 4y + 3$

   C. $-5y^3 + y^2 + 4y + 3$

   D. $-5y^3 + 5y^2 + 4y - 3$

4. Solve $x^3 = 343$.

   A. 6   C. 8

   B. 7   D. 9

5. One online seller has about 6×10^8 online orders, and another online seller has about 5×10^7 online orders. How many times more orders does the first company have?

   A. 12   C. 20

   B. 15   D. 32

6. Simplify $\frac{x^2 y^{-2}}{x^{-3} y^3}$.

   A. $\frac{x^5}{y^5}$ C. $\frac{1}{x^5 y^5}$

   B. $\frac{y^5}{x^5}$ D. $x^5 y^5$

7. What is 15% of 64?

   A. 5:48   C. 48:5

   B. 15:64   D. 64:15

8. Which number satisfies the proportion $\frac{378}{?} = \frac{18}{7}$?

   A. 18   C. 972

   B. 147   D. 2,646

9. If a tree grows an average of 4.2 inches in a day, what is the rate of change in its height per month? Assume a month is 30 days.

   A. 0.14 inches per month   C. 34.2 inches per month

   B. 4.2 inches per month   D. 126 inches per month

10. Solve the equation by the quadratic formula, $11x^2 - 14x + 4 = 0$.

    A. -0.84 and -0.43 C. -0.84 and 0.43

    B. 0.84 and -0.43 D. 0.84 and 0.43

11. Solve the equation by any method, $3x^2 - 5 = 22$.

    A. 0   C. ± 2

    B. ± 1 D. ± 3

12. Solve the equation by the square root method, $5x^2 + 10 = 10$.

    A. 0   C. 2

    B. 1   D. 3

CHAPTER 7 FUNCTIONS
PRACTICE QUIZ – ANSWER KEY

1. A. The correct solution is $x^3 + x^2 + x - 3$.

$(x{-}1)(x^2 + 2x + 3) = (x{-}1)(x^2) + (x{-}1)(2x) + (x{-}1)(3) = x^3 - x^2 + 2x^2 - 2x + 3x - 3 = x^3 + x^2 + x - 3$

See Lesson: Polynomials.

2. B. The correct solution is $(3x{-}5)^2$. The expression $9x^2 - 30x + 25$ is rewritten as $(3x{-}5)^2$ because the value of a is $3x$ and the value of b is 5. **See Lesson: Polynomials.**

3. D. The correct solution is $-5y^3 + 5y^2 + 4y - 3$.

$(3y^2 + 4y){-}(5y^3 - 2y^2 + 3) = (3y^2 + 4y) + (-5y^3 + 2y^2 - 3) = -5y^3 + (3y^2 + 2y^2) + 4y - 3 = -5y^3 + 5y^2 + 4y - 3$

See Lesson: Polynomials.

4. B. The correct solution is 7 because the cube root of 343 is 7. **See Lesson: Powers, Exponents, Roots, and Radicals.**

5. A. The correct solution is 12 because the first company has about 600,000,000 orders and the second company has about 50,000,000 orders. So, the first company is about 12 times larger. **See Lesson: Powers, Exponents, Roots, and Radicals.**

6. A. The correct solution is $\frac{x^5}{y^5}$ because $\frac{x^2 y^{-2}}{x^{-3} y^3} = x^{2-(-3)} y^{-2-3} = x^5 y^{-5} = \frac{x^5}{y^5}$. **See Lesson: Powers, Exponents, Roots, and Radicals.**

7. C. Either set up a proportion or just note that this question is asking for a fraction of a specific number: 15% (or $\frac{3}{20}$) of 64. Multiply $\frac{3}{20}$ by 64 to get $\frac{48}{5}$, or 48:5. **See Lesson: Ratios, Proportions, and Percentages.**

8. B. The number 147 satisfies the proportion. First, divide 378 by 18 to get 21. Then, multiply 21 by 7 to get 147. Check your answer by dividing 147 by 7: the quotient is also 21, so 147 satisfies the proportion. **See Lesson: Ratios, Proportions, and Percentages.**

9. D. The rate of change is 126 inches per month. One approach is to set up a proportion.

$$\frac{1 \text{ day}}{4.2 \text{ inches}} = \frac{30 \text{ days}}{?}$$

Since 1 month is equivalent to 30 days, multiply the rate of change per day by 30 to get the rate of change per month. 4.2 inches multiplied by 30 is 126 inches. Thus, the growth rate is 126 inches per month. **See Lesson: Ratios, Proportions, and Percentages.**

10. D. The correct solutions are 0.84 and 0.43.

$$x = \frac{-(-14) \pm \sqrt{(-14)^2 - 4(11)(4)}}{2(11)}$$ Substitute 11 for a, –14 for b, and 4 for c.

$$x = \frac{14 \pm \sqrt{196 - 176}}{22}$$ Apply the exponent and perform the multiplication.

$$x = \frac{14 \pm \sqrt{20}}{22}$$ Perform the subtraction.

$$x = \frac{14 \pm 4.47}{22}$$ Apply the square root.

$$x = \frac{14 + 4.47}{22}, \ x = \frac{14 - 4.47}{22}$$ Separate the problem into two expressions.

$$x = \frac{18.47}{22} = 0.84, \ x = \frac{9.53}{22} = 0.43$$ Simplify the numerator and divide.

See Lesson: Solving Quadratic Equations.

11. D. The correct solutions are ±3. Solve this equation by the square root method.

$3x^2 = 27$	Add 5 to both sides of the equation.
$x^2 = \pm 9$	Divide both sides of the equation by 3.
$x = \pm 3$	Apply the square root to both sides of the equation.

See Lesson: Solving Quadratic Equations.

12. A. The correct solution is 0.

$5x^2 = 0$	Subtract 10 from both sides of the equation.
$x^2 = 0$	Divide both sides of the equation by 5.
$x = 0$	Apply the square root to both sides of the equation.

See Lesson: Solving Quadratic Equations.

CHAPTER 8 GEOMETRY

CONGRUENCE

This lesson discusses basic terms for geometry. Many polygons have the property of lines of symmetry, or rotational symmetry. Rotations, reflections, and translations are ways to create congruent polygons.

Geometry Terms

The terms *point*, *line*, and *plane* help define other terms in geometry. A point is an exact location in space with no size and has a label with a capital letter. A line has location and direction, is always straight, and has infinitely many points that extend in both directions. A plane has infinitely many intersecting lines that extend forever in all directions.

The diagram shows point W, point X, point Y, and point Z. The line is labeled as $\overleftrightarrow{WX}$, and the plane is Plane A or Plane WYZ (or any three points in the plane).

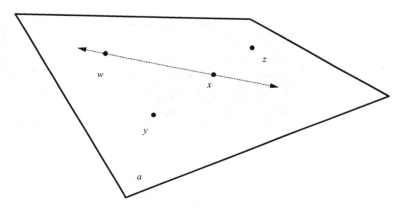

With these definitions, many other geometry terms can be defined. *Collinear* is a term for points that lie on the same line, and *coplanar* is a term for points and/or lines within the same plane. A line segment is a part of a line with two endpoints. For example, $\overline{WX}$ has endpoints W and X. A ray has an endpoint and extends forever in one direction. For example, $\overrightarrow{AB}$ has an endpoint of A, and $\overrightarrow{BA}$ has an endpoint of B. The intersection of lines, planes, segment, or rays is a point or a set of points.

Some key statements that are evident in geometry are

- There is exactly one straight line through any two points.
- There is exactly one plane that contains any three non-collinear points.
- A line with points in the plane lies in the plane.
- Two lines intersect at a point.
- Two planes intersect at a line.

Two rays that share an endpoint form an angle. The vertex is the common endpoint of the two rays that form an angle. When naming an angle, the vertex is the center point. The angle below is named $\angle ABC$ or $\angle CBA$.

An acute angle has a measure between 0° and 90°, and a 90° angle is a right angle. An obtuse angle has a measure between 90° and 180°, and a 180° angle is a straight angle.

There are two special sets of lines. Parallel lines are at least two lines that never intersect within the same plane. Perpendicular lines intersect at one point and form four angles.

Example

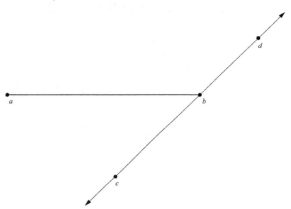

BE CAREFUL!

Lines are always named with two points, a plane can be named with three points, and an angle is named with the vertex as the center point.

Describe the diagram.

A. Points A, B, C, and D are collinear.

B. Points A, C, and D are collinear.

C. $\overline{CD}$ intersects $\overleftrightarrow{AB}$ at point B.

D. $\overline{AB}$ intersects $\overleftrightarrow{CD}$ at point B.

The correct answer is **D**. The correct solution is $\overline{AB}$ intersects $\overleftrightarrow{CD}$ at point B. The segment intersects the line at point B.

Line and Rotational Symmetry

Symmetry is a reflection or rotation of a shape that allows that shape to be carried onto itself. Line symmetry, or reflection symmetry, is when two halves of a shape are reflected onto each other across a line. A shape may have none, one, or several lines of symmetry. A kite has one line of symmetry, and a scalene triangle has no lines of symmetry.

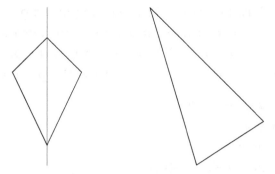

Rotational symmetry is when a figure can be mapped onto itself by a rotation about a point through any angle between 0° and 360°. The order of rotational symmetry is the number of times the object can be rotated. If there is no rotational symmetry, the order is 1 because the object can only be rotated 360° to map the figure onto itself. A square has 90° rotational symmetry and is order 4 because it can be rotated 90°, 180°, 270°, and 360°. A trapezoid has no rotational symmetry and is order 1 because it can only be rotated 360° to map onto itself.

KEEP IN MIND

A polygon can have both, neither, or either reflection and rotational symmetry.

Example

What is the rotational symmetry for a regular octagon?

A. 30°   B. 45°   C. 60°   D. 75°

The correct answer is **B**. The correct solution is 45°. For a regular polygon, divide 360° by the eight sides of the octagon to obtain 45°.

Rotations, Reflections, and Translations

There are three types of transformations: rotations, reflections, and translations. A rotation is a turn of a figure about a point in a given direction. A reflection is a flip over a line of symmetry, and a translation is a slide horizontally, vertically, or both. Each of these transformations produces a congruent image.

A rotation changes ordered pairs (x, y) in the coordinate plane. A 90° rotation counterclockwise about the point becomes $(-y, x)$, a 180° rotation counterclockwise about the point becomes $(-x, -y)$, and a 270° rotation the point becomes $(y, -x)$. Using the point (6, −8),

- 90° rotation counterclockwise about the origin (8, 6)
- 180° rotation counterclockwise about the origin (−6, 8)
- 270° rotation counterclockwise about the origin (−8, −6)

A reflection also changes ordered pairs (x, y) in the coordinate plane. A reflection across the x-axis changes the sign of the y-coordinate, and a reflection across the y-axis changes the sign of the x-coordinate. A reflection over the line $y = x$ changes the points to (y, x), and a reflection over the line $y = -x$ changes the points to $(-y, -x)$. Using the point $(6, -8)$,

- A reflection across the x-axis $(6, 8)$
- A reflection across the y-axis $(-6, -8)$
- A reflection over the line $y = x$ $(-8, 6)$
- A reflection over the line $y = -x$ $(8, -6)$

A translation changes ordered pairs (x, y) left or right and/or up or down. Adding a positive value to an x-coordinate is a translation to the right, and adding a negative value to an x-coordinate is a translation to the left. Adding a positive value to a y-coordinate is a translation up, and adding a negative value to a y-coordinate is a translation down. Using the point $(6, -8)$,

KEEP IN MIND

A rotation is a turn, a reflection is a flip, and a translation is a slide.

- A translation of $(x + 3)$ is a translation right 3 units $(9, -8)$
- A translation of $(x - 3)$ is a translation left 3 units $(3, -8)$
- A translation of $(y + 3)$ is a translation up 3 units $(6, -5)$
- A translation of $(y - 3)$ is a translation down 3 units $(6, -11)$

Example

$\triangle ABC$ has points A $(3, -2)$, B $(2, -1)$, and C $(-1, 4)$, which after a transformation become A' $(2, 3)$, B' $(1, 2)$, and C' $(-4, -1)$. What is the transformation between the points?

A. Reflection across the x-axis

B. Reflection across the y-axis

C. Rotation of 90° counterclockwise

D. Rotation of 270° counterclockwise

The correct answer is **C**. The correct solution is a rotation of 90° counterclockwise because the points (x, y) become $(y, -x)$.

Let's Review!

- The terms *point*, *line*, and *plane* help define many terms in geometry.
- Symmetry allows a figure to carry its shape onto itself. This can be reflectional or rotational symmetry.
- Three transformations are rotation (turn), reflection (flip), and translation (slide).

SIMILARITY, RIGHT TRIANGLES, AND TRIGONOMETRY

This lesson defines and applies terminology associated with coordinate planes. It also demonstrates how to find the area of two-dimensional shapes and the surface area and volume of three-dimensional cubes and right prisms.

Coordinate Plane

The **coordinate plane** is a two-dimensional number line with the horizontal axis called the **x-axis** and the vertical axis called the **y-axis**. Each **ordered pair** or **coordinate** is listed as (x, y). The center point is the origin and has an ordered pair of (0, 0). A coordinate plane has four quadrants.

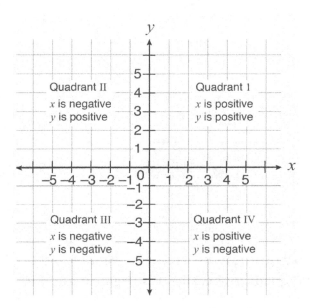

KEEP IN MIND

The *x*-coordinates are positive to the right of the *y*-axis. The *y*-coordinates are positive above the *x*-axis.

To graph a point in the coordinate plane, start with the x-coordinate. This point states the number of steps to the left (negative) or to the right (positive) from the origin. Then, the y-coordinate states the number of steps up (positive) or down (negative) from the x-coordinate.

Given a set of ordered pairs, points can be drawn in the coordinate plane to create polygons. The length of a segment can be found if the segment has the same first coordinate or the same second coordinate.

Volume of a Sphere

A **sphere** is a round, three-dimensional solid, with every point on its surface equidistant to the center. The formula for the volume of a sphere is represented by just the radius of the sphere. The volume of a sphere is $V = \frac{4}{3}\pi r^3$. The volume of a hemi (half) of a sphere is $V = \left(\frac{1}{2}\right)\frac{4}{3}\pi r^3 = \frac{2}{3}\pi r^3$.

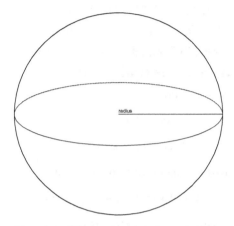

BE CAREFUL!
The radius is cubed, not squared, for the volume of a sphere.

Example

A sphere has a radius of 3 centimeters. Find the volume of a sphere in cubic centimeters.

A. 18π B. 27π C. 36π D. 45π

The correct answer is **C**. The correct solution is 36π. Substitute the values into the formula and simplify using the order of operations, $V = \frac{4}{3}\pi r^3 = \frac{4}{3}\pi 3^3 = \frac{4}{3}\pi(27) = 36\pi$ cubic centimeters.

Let's Review!

- The volume is the capacity of a three-dimensional object and is expressed in cubic units.
- The volume formula for a cylinder is the product of the area of the base (which is a circle) and the height of the cylinder.
- The volume formula for a pyramid or cone is one-third of the product of the area of the base (a circle in the case of the cone) and the height of the pyramid or cone.
- The volume formula for a sphere is $V = \frac{4}{3}\pi r^3$.

CHAPTER 8 GEOMETRY PRACTICE QUIZ

1. The bottom of a plastic pool has an area of 64 square feet. What is the radius to the nearest tenth of a foot? Use 3.14 for π.

   A. 2.3

   B. 4.5

   C. 6.9

   D. 10.2

2. The area of a circular hand mirror is 200 square centimeters. Find the circumference of the mirror to the nearest tenth of a centimeter. Use 3.14 for π.

   A. 25.1

   B. 50.2

   C. 75.3

   D. 100.4

3. The circumference of a pie is 300 centimeters. Find the area of one-fourth of the pie to the nearest tenth of a square centimeter. Use 3.14 for π.

   A. 1,793.6

   B. 2,284.8

   C. 7,174.4

   D. 14,348.8

4. A regular hexagon has a rotational order of 6. What is the smallest number of degrees for the figure to be rotated onto itself?

   A. 30°

   B. 60°

   C. 90°

   D. 120°

5. $\triangle GHI$ has points G (2, 7), H (−3, −8), and I (−6, 0). After a transformation, the points are G' (7, 2), H' (−8, −3), and I' (0, −6). What is the transformation between the points?

   A. Reflection across the x-axis

   B. Reflection across the y-axis

   C. Reflection across the line of $y = x$

   D. Reflection across the line of $y = -x$

6. Name the right angle in the diagram.

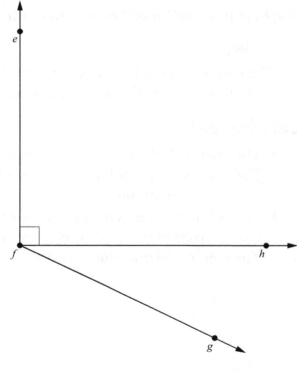

   A. ∠EHF

   B. ∠EFG

   C. ∠EFH

   D. ∠EGF

7. The volume of a cone is 28π cubic inches, and its diameter is 2 inches. What is the height of the cone?

   A. 2 inches
   B. 4 inches
   C. 6 inches
   D. 8 inches

8. A hemi-sphere has a radius of 6 centimeters. Find the volume in cubic centimeters.

   A. 72π
   B. 144π
   C. 288π
   D. 576π

9. A rectangular pyramid has a height of 7 meters and a volume of 112 cubic meters. Find the area of the base in square meters.

   A. 16
   B. 28
   C. 42
   D. 48

10. A right rectangular prism has dimensions of 3 inches by 6 inches by 9 inches. What is the surface area in square inches?

    A. 162
    B. 198
    C. 232
    D. 286

11. A right triangle has a base of 6 inches and a hypotenuse of 10 inches. Find the height in inches of the triangle if the area is 24 square inches.

    A. 4
    B. 6
    C. 8
    D. 10

12. **Draw a rectangle with the coordinates (5,7), (5,1), (1,1), (1,7).**

A.

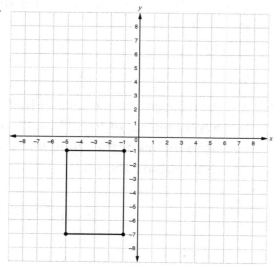

C.

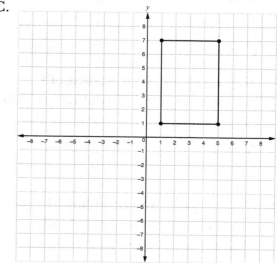

B.

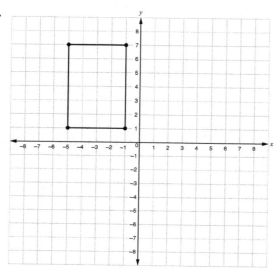

D.

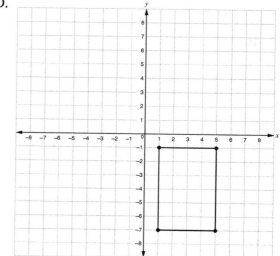

CHAPTER 8 GEOMETRY PRACTICE QUIZ – ANSWER KEY

1. B. The correct solution is 4.5 because $A = \pi r^2$; $64 = 3.14 r^2$; $20.38 = r^2$; $r \approx 4.5$ feet. **See Lesson: Circles.**

2. B. The correct solution is 50.2. $A = \pi r^2$; $200 = 3.14 r^2$; $63.69 = r^2$; $r \approx 8.0$ centimeters. $C = 2\pi r$; $C = 2(3.14)8.0 \approx 50.2$ centimeters. **See Lesson: Circles.**

3. A. The correct solution is 1,793.6. $C = 2\pi r$; $300 = 2(3.14)r$; $300 = 6.28r$; $r \approx 47.8$ centimeters. $A = \frac{1}{4}\pi r^2 \approx \frac{1}{4}(3.14)(47.8)^2 \approx \frac{1}{4}3.14(2,284.84) \approx 1793.6$ square centimeters. **See Lesson: Circles.**

4. B. The correct solution is 60°. For a regular hexagon, divide 360° by the six sides to obtain 60°. **See Lesson: Congruence.**

5. C. The correct solution is a reflection across the line of $y = x$ because the points (x, y) become (y, x). **See Lesson: Congruence.**

6. C. The correct solution is $\angle EFH$ because the vertex of the right angle is F and the other two points are E and H. **See Lesson: Congruence.**

7. C. The correct solution is 6 inches. Substitute the values into the formula, $2\pi = \frac{1}{3}\pi(1)^2 h$ and simplify using the right side of the equation by applying the exponent and multiplying, $2\pi = \frac{1}{3}\pi(1)h$, $2\pi = \frac{1}{3}\pi h$. Multiply both sides of the equation by 3 to get a solution of 6 inches. **See Lesson: Measurement and Dimension.**

8. B. The correct solution is 144π. Substitute the values into the formula and simplify using the order of operations, $V = \frac{2}{3}\pi r^3 = \frac{2}{3}\pi(6^3) = \frac{2}{3}\pi(216) = 144\pi$ cubic centimeters. **See Lesson: Measurement and Dimension.**

9. D. The correct solution is 48. Substitute the values into the formula, $112 = \frac{1}{3}B(7)$ and simplify the right side of the equation, $112 = \frac{7}{3}B$. Multiply both sides of the equation by the reciprocal, $B = 48$ square meters. **See Lesson: Measurement and Dimension.**

10. B. The correct solution is 198. Substitute the values into the formula and simplify using the order of operations, $SA = 2lw + 2lh + 2hw = 2(3)(6) + 2(6)(9) + 2(9)(3) = 36 + 108 + 54 = 198$ square inches. **See Lesson: Similarity, Right Triangles, and Trigonometry.**

11. C. The correct solution is 8. Substitute the values into the formula, $24 = \frac{1}{2}(6)h$ and simplify the right side of the equation, $24 = 3h$. Divide both sides of the equation by 3, $h = 8$ inches. **See Lesson: Similarity, Right Triangles, and Trigonometry.**

12. C. All points are in the first quadrant. **See Lesson: Similarity, Right Triangles, and Trigonometry.**

CHAPTER 9 STATISTICS AND PROBABILITY

INTERPRETING GRAPHICS

This lesson discusses how to create a bar, line, and circle graph and how to interpret data from these graphs. It also explores how to calculate and interpret the measures of central tendency.

Creating a Line, Bar, and Circle Graph

A line graph is a graph with points connected by segments that examines changes over time. The horizontal axis contains the independent variable (the input value), which is usually time. The vertical axis contains the dependent variable (the output value), which is an item that measures a quantity. A line graph will have a title and an appropriate scale to display the data. The graph can include more than one line.

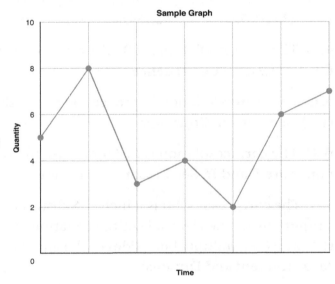

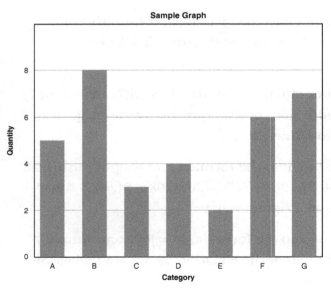

A bar graph uses rectangular horizontal or vertical bars to display information. A bar graph has categories on the horizontal axis and the quantity on the vertical axis. Bar graphs need a title and an appropriate scale for the frequency. The graph can include more than one bar.

BE CAREFUL

Make sure to use the appropriate scale for each type of graph.

A circle graph is a circular chart that is divided into parts, and each part shows the relative size of the value. To create a circle graph, find the total number and divide each part by the total to find the percentage. Then, to find the part of the circle, multiply each percent by 360°. Draw each part of the circle and create a title.

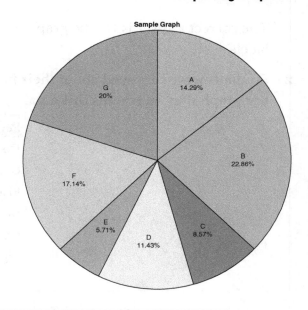

Sample Graph

Examples

1. **The table shows the amount of rainfall in inches. Select the line graph that represents this data.**

Day	1	2	3	4	5	6	7	8	9	10	11	12
Rainfall Amount	0.5	0.2	0.4	1.1	1.6	0.9	0.7	1.3	1.5	0.8	0.5	0.1

A.

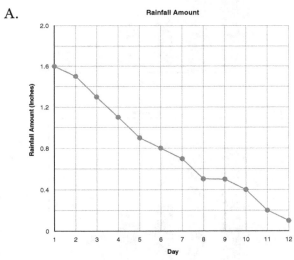

C.

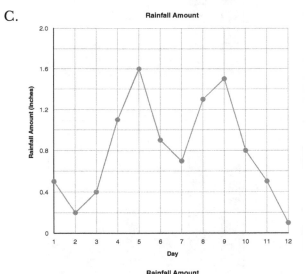

B.

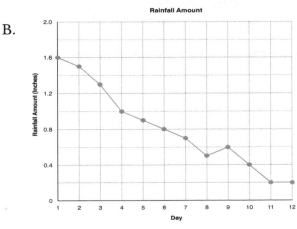

D.

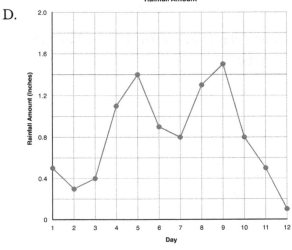

The correct answer is **C**. The graph is displayed correctly for the days with the appropriate labels.

2. **Students were surveyed about their favorite pet, and the table shows the results. Select the bar graph that represents this data.**

Pet	Quantity
Dog	14
Cat	16
Fish	4
Bird	8
Gerbil	7
Pig	3

A.
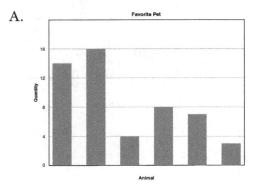

C.
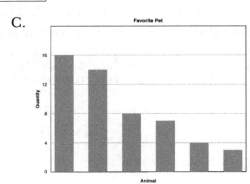

B.
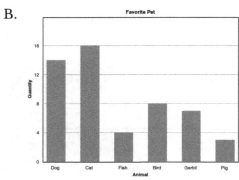

D.
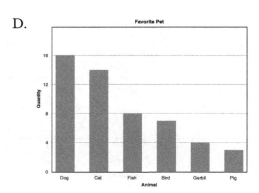

The correct answer is **B**. The bar graph represents each pet correctly and is labeled correctly.

3. The table shows the amount a family spends each month. Select the circle graph that represents the data.

Item	Food/Household Items	Bills	Mortgage	Savings	Miscellaneous
Amount	$700	$600	$400	$200	$100

A.

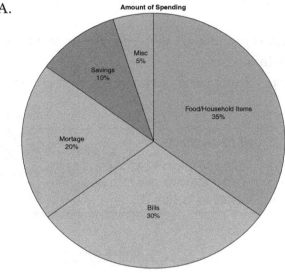

C.

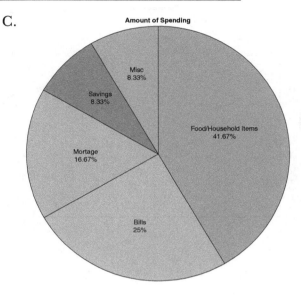

B.

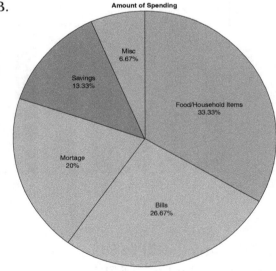

D.

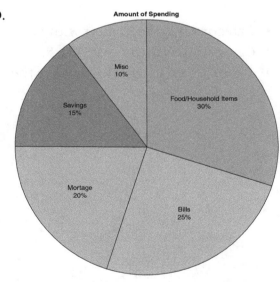

The correct answer is **A**. The total amount spent each month is $2,000. The section of the circle for food and household items is $\frac{700}{2,000} = 0.35 = 35\%$. The section of the circle for bills is $\frac{600}{2,000} = 0.30 = 30\%$. The section of the circle for mortgage is $\frac{400}{2,000} = 0.20 = 20\%$. The section of the circle for savings is $\frac{200}{2,000} = 0.10 = 10\%$. The section of the circle for miscellaneous is $\frac{100}{2,000} = 0.05 = 5\%$.

Interpreting and Evaluating Line, Bar, and Circle Graphs

Graph and charts are used to create visual examples of information, and it is important to be able to interpret them. The examples from Section 1 can show a variety of conclusions.

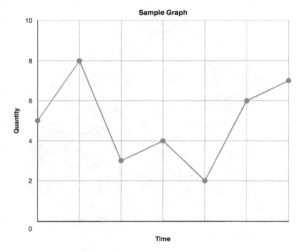

- The minimum value is 2, and the maximum value is 8.
- The largest decrease is between the second and third points.
- The largest increase is between the fifth and sixth points.

KEEP IN MIND

Read and determine the parts of the graph before answering questions related to the graph.

- Category B is the highest with 8.
- Category E is the lowest with 2.
- There are no categories that are the same.

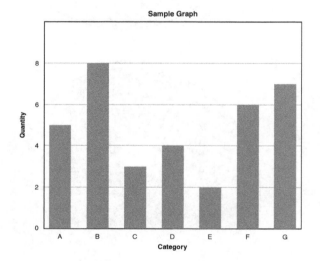

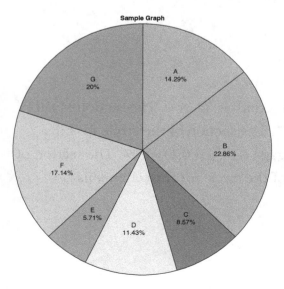

- Category B is the largest with 22.86%.
- Category E is the smallest with 5.71%.
- All of the categories are less than one-fourth of the graph.

Examples

1. **The line chart shows the number of minutes a commuter drove to work during a month. Which statement is true for the line chart?**

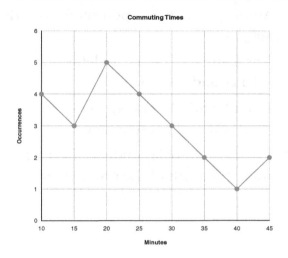

A. The commuter drove 25 minutes to work the most times

B. The commuter drove 25 minutes to work the fewest times.

C. The commuter took 10 minutes and 25 minutes twice during the month.

D. The commuter took 35 minutes and 45 minutes twice during the month.

The correct answer is **D**. The commuter took 35 minutes and 45 minutes twice during the month.

2. **The bar chart shows the distance different families traveled for summer vacation. Which statement is true for the bar chart?**

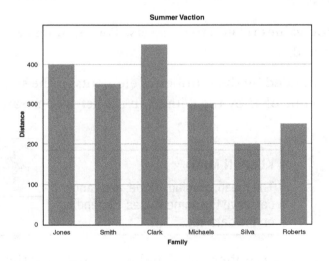

A. All families drove more than 200 miles.

B. The Clark family traveled 250 miles more than the Silva family.

C. The Roberts family traveled more miles than the Michaels family.

D. The Jones family is the only family that traveled 400 miles or more.

The correct answer is **B**. The correct solution is the Clark family traveled 250 miles more than the Silva family. The Clark family traveled 450 miles, and the Silva family traveled 200 miles, making the difference 250 miles.

3. Students were interviewed about their favorite subject in school. The circle graph shows the results. Which statement is true for the circle graph?

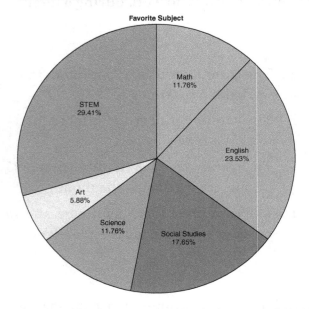

Favorite Subject

A. Math is the smallest percent for favorite subject.

B. The same number of students favor science and social studies.

C. English and STEM together are more than half of the respondents.

D. English and social students together are more than half of the respondents.

The correct answer is **C**. The correct solution is English and STEM together are more than half of the respondents because these values are more than 50% combined.

Mean, Median, Mode, and Range

The mean, median, mode, and range are common values related to data sets. These values can be calculated using the data set 2, 4, 7, 6, 8, 5, 6, and 3.

The mean is the sum of all numbers in a data set divided by the number of elements in the set. The sum of items in the data set is 41. Divide the value of 41 by the 8 items in the set. The mean is 5.125.

The median is the middle number of a data set when written in order. If there are an odd number of items, the median is the middle number. If there are an even number of items, the median is the mean of the middle two numbers. The

> **KEEP IN MIND**
> The mean, median, mode, and range can have the same values, depending on the data set.

numbers in order are 2, 3, 4, 5, 6, 6, 7, 8. The middle two numbers are 5 and 6. The mean of the two middle numbers is 5.5, which is the median.

The mode is the number or numbers that occur most often. There can be no modes, one mode, or many modes. In the data set, the number 6 appears twice, making 6 the mode.

The range is the difference between the highest and lowest values in a data set. The highest value is 8 and the lowest value is 2, for a range of 6.

Examples

1. Find the mean and the median for the data set 10, 20, 40, 20, 30, 50, 40, 60, 30, 10, 40, 20, 50, 70, and 80.

   A. The mean is 40, and the median is 38.

   B. The mean is 38, and the median is 40.

   C. The mean is 36, and the median is 50.

   D. The mean is 50, and the median is 36.

   The correct answer is **B.** The correct solution is the mean is 38 and the median is 40. The sum of all items is 570 divided by 15, which is 38. The data set in order is 10, 10, 20, 20, 20, 30, 30, 40, 40, 40, 50, 50, 60, 70, 80. The median number is 40.

2. Find the mode and the range for the data set 10, 20, 40, 20, 30, 50, 40, 60, 30, 10, 40, 20, 50, 70, and 80.

   A. The mode is 20, and the range is 70.

   B. The mode is 40, and the range is 70.

   C. The modes are 20 and 40, and the range is 70.

   D. The modes are 20, 40, and 70, and the range is 70.

   The correct answer is **C.** The correct solution is the modes are 20 and 40 and the range is 70. The modes are 20 and 40 because each of these numbers appears three times. The range is the difference between 80 and 10, which is 70.

Let's Review!

- A bar graph, line graph, and circle graph are different ways to summarize and represent data.
- The mean, median, mode, and range are values that can be used to interpret the meaning of a set of numbers.

STATISTICAL MEASURES

This lesson explores the different sampling techniques using random and non-random sampling. The lesson also distinguishes among different study techniques. In addition, it provides simulations that compare results with expected outcomes.

Probability and Non-Probability Sampling

A population includes all items within a set of data, while a sample consists of one or more observations from a population.

The collection of data samples from a population is an important part of research and helps researcher draw conclusions related to populations. Probability sampling creates a sample from a population by using random sampling techniques.

KEEP IN MIND
Probability sampling is random, and non-probability sampling is not random.

Every person within a population has an equal chance of being selected for a sample. Non-probability sampling creates a sample from a population without using random sampling techniques.

There are four types of probability sampling. Simple random sampling is assigning a number to each member of a population and randomly selecting numbers. Stratified sampling uses simple random sampling after the population is split into equal groups. Systematic sampling chooses every n^{th} member from a list or a group. Cluster random sampling uses natural groups in a population: the population is divided into groups, and random samples are collected from groups.

Each type of probability sampling has an advantage and a disadvantage when finding an appropriate sample.

Probability Sampling	Advantage	Disadvantage
Simple random sampling	Most cases have a sample representative of a population	Not efficient for large samples
Stratified random sampling	Creates layers of random samples from different groups representative of a population	Not efficient for large samples
Systematic sampling	Creates a sample representative of population without a random number selection	Not as random as simple random sampling
Cluster random sampling	Relatively easy and convenient to implement	Might not work if clusters are different from one another

There are four types of non-probability sampling. Convenience sampling produces samples that are easy to access. Volunteer sampling asks for volunteers or recommendations for a sample. Purposive sampling bases samples on specific characteristics by selecting samples from a group that meets the qualifications of the study. Quota sampling is choosing samples of groups of the subpopulation.

Examples

1. **A factory is studying the quality of beverage samples. There are 50 bottles randomly chosen from one shipment every 60 minutes. What type of sampling is used?**

   A. Systematic sampling

   B. Simple random sampling

   C. Cluster random sampling

   D. Stratified random sampling

   The correct answer is **C**. The correct solution is cluster random sampling because bottles of beverage are selected within specific boundaries.

2. **A group conducting a survey asks a person for his or her opinion. Then, the group asks the person being surveyed for the names of 10 friends to obtain additional options. What type of sampling is used?**

   A. Quota sampling

   B. Volunteer sampling

   C. Purposive sampling

   D. Convenience sampling

   The correct answer is **B**. The correct solution is volunteer sampling because the group is looking for recommendations.

Census, Surveys, Experiments, Observational Studies

Various sampling techniques are used to collect data from a population. These are in the form of a census, a survey, observational studies, or experiments.

A census collects data by asking everyone in a population the same question. Asking everyone at school or everyone at work are examples of a

KEEP IN MIND

A census includes everyone within a population, and a survey includes every subject of a sample. An observational study involves watching groups randomly, and an experiment involves assigning groups.

census. A survey collects data on every subject within a sample. The subjects can be determined by convenience sampling or by simple random sampling. Examples of surveys are asking sophomores at school or first shift workers at work.

In an observational study, data collection occurs by watching or observing an event. Watching children who play outside and observing if they drink water or sports drinks is an example. An experiment is way of finding information by assigning people to groups and collecting data on observations. Assigning one group of children to drink water and another group to drink sports drinks after playing and making comparisons is an example of an experiment.

Examples

1. **A school wants to create a census to identify students' favorite subject in school. Which group should the school ask?**

    A. All staff

    C. All sophomores

    B. All students

    D. All male students

    The correct answer is **B.** The correct solution is all students because this gathers information on the entire population.

2. **A researcher records the arrival time of employees at a job based on their actual start time. What type of study is this?**

    A. Census

    C. Experiment

    B. Survey

    D. Observational study

    The correct answer is **D.** The correct solution is observational study because the researcher is observing the time the employees arrive at work.

3. **The local county wants to test the water quality of a stream by collecting samples. What should the county collect?**

    A. The water quality at one spot

    C. The water quality under bridges

    B. The water quality under trees

    D. The water quality at different spots

    The correct answer is **D.** The correct solution is the water quality at different spots because this survey allows for the collection of different samples.

Simulations

A simulation enables researchers to study real-world events by modeling events. Advantages of simulations are that they are quick, easy, and inexpensive; the disadvantage is that the results are approximations. The steps to complete a simulation are as follows:

KEEP IN MIND

A simulation is only useful if the results closely mirror real-world outcomes.

*   Describe the outcomes.
*   Assign a random value to the outcomes.
*   Choose a source to generate the outcomes.
*   Generate values for the outcomes until a consistent pattern emerges.
*   Analyze the results.

Examples

1. A family has two children and wants to simulate the gender of the children. Which object would be beneficial to use for the simulation?

   A. Coin

   B. Four-section spinner

   C. Six-sided number cube

   D. Random number generator

   The correct answer is **B**. The correct solution is a four-section spinner because there are four possible outcomes of the event (boy/boy, boy/girl, girl/boy, and girl/girl).

2. There are six options from which to choose a meal at a festival. A model using a six-sided number cube is used to represent the simulation.

Hamburger	Chicken	Hot Dog	Bratwurst	Pork Chop	Fish	Total
1	2	3	4	5	6	
83	82	85	89	86	75	500

   Choose the statement that correctly answers whether the simulation of using a six-sided number cube is consistent with the actual number of dinners sold and then explains why or why not.

   A. The simulation is consistent because it has six equally likely outcomes.

   B. The simulation is consistent because it has two equally likely outcomes.

   C. The simulation is not consistent because of the limited number of outcomes.

   D. The simulation is not consistent because of the unlimited number of outcomes.

   The correct answer is **A**. The correct solution is the simulation is consistent because it has six equally likely outcomes. The six-sided number cube provides consistent outcomes because there is an equal opportunity to select any dinner.

Let's Review!

- Probability (random) sampling and non-probability (not random) sampling are ways to collect data.
- Censuses, surveys, experiments, and observational studies are ways to collect data from a population.
- A simulation is way to model random events and compare the results to real-world outcomes.

STATISTICS & PROBABILITY: THE RULES OF PROBABILITY

This lesson explores a sample space and its outcomes and provides an introduction to probability, including how to calculate expected values and analyze decisions based on probability.

Sample Space

A **sample space** is the set of all possible outcomes. Using a deck of cards labeled 1–10, the sample space is 1, 2, 3, 4, 5, 6, 7, 8, 9, and 10. An **event** is a subset of the sample space. For example, if a card is drawn and the outcome of the event is an even number, possible results are 2, 4, 6, 8, 10.

The **union** of two events is everything in both events, and the notation is $A \cup B$. The union of events is associated with the word *or*. For example, a card is drawn that is either a multiple of 3 or a multiple of 4. The set containing the multiples of 3 is 3, 6, and 9. The set containing the multiples of 4 is 4 and 8. The union of the set is 3, 4, 6, 8, and 9.

The **intersection** of two events is all of the events in both sets, and the notation is $A \cap B$. The intersection of events is associated with the word *and*. For example, a card is drawn that is even and a multiple of 4. The set containing even numbers is 2, 4, 6, 8, and 10. The set containing the multiples of 4 is 4 and 8. The intersection is 4 and 8 because these numbers are in both sets.

The **complement** of an event is an outcome that is not part of the set. The complement of an event is associated with the word *not*. A card is drawn and is not a multiple of 5. The set not containing multiples of 5 is 1, 2, 3, 4, 6, 7, 8, and 9. The complement of not a multiple of 5 is 1, 2, 3, 4, 6, 7, 8, and 9.

Examples

Use the following table of the results when rolling two six-sided number cubes.

1, 1	1, 2	1, 3	1, 4	1, 5	1, 6
2, 1	2, 2	2, 3	2, 4	2, 5	2, 6
3, 1	3, 2	3, 3	3, 4	3, 5	3, 6
4, 1	4, 2	4, 3	4, 4	4, 5	4, 6
5, 1	5, 2	5, 3	5, 4	5, 5	5, 6
6, 1	6, 2	6, 3	6, 4	6, 5	6, 6

1. **How many possible outcomes are there for the union of rolling a sum of 3 or a sum of 5?**

   A. 2   B. 4   C. 6   D. 8

   The correct answer is **C**. The correct solution is 6 possible outcomes. There are two options for the first event (2, 1) and (1, 2). There are 4 options for the second event (4, 1), (3, 2), (2, 3), and (1, 4). The union of two events is six possible outcomes.

2. **How many possible outcomes are there for the intersection of rolling a double and a multiple of 3?**

   A. 0   B. 2   C. 4   D. 6

   The correct answer is **B**. The correct solution is 2 possible outcomes. There are six options for the first event (1, 1), (2, 2), (3, 3), (4, 4), (5, 5), and (6, 6). There are 12 options for the second event of the multiple of three. The intersection is (3, 3) and (6, 6) because these numbers meet both requirements.

3. **How many possible outcomes are there for the complement of rolling a 3 and a 5?**

   A. 16   B. 18   C. 27   D. 36

   The correct answer is **A**. The correct solution is 16 possible outcomes. There are 16 options of not rolling a 3 or a 5.

Probability

The **probability** of an event is the number of favorable outcomes divided by the total number of possible outcomes.

$$Probability = \frac{number\ of\ favorable\ outcomes}{number\ of\ possible\ outcomes}$$

BE CAREFUL!

Make sure that you apply the correct formula for the probability of an event.

Probability is a value between 0 (event does not happen) and 1 (event will happen). For example, the probability of getting heads when a coin is flipped is $\frac{1}{2}$ because heads is 1 option out of 2 possibilities. The probability of rolling an odd number on a six-sided number cube is $\frac{3}{6} = \frac{1}{2}$ because there are three odd numbers, 1, 3, and 5, out of 6 possible numbers.

The probability of an "or" event happening is the sum of the events happening. For example, the probability of rolling an odd number or a 4 on a six-sided number cube is $\frac{4}{6}$. The probability of rolling an odd number is $\frac{3}{6}$, and the probability of rolling a 4 is $\frac{1}{6}$. Therefore, the probability is $\frac{3}{6} + \frac{1}{6} = \frac{4}{6} = \frac{2}{3}$.

The probability of an "and" event happening is the product of the probability of two or more events. The probability of rolling 6 three times in a row is $\frac{1}{216}$. The probability of a single event is $\frac{1}{6}$, and this fraction is multiplied three times to find the probability, $\frac{1}{6} \times \frac{1}{6} \times \frac{1}{6}$. There are cases of "with replacement" when the item is returned to the pile and "without replacement" when the item is not returned to the pile.

The probability of a "not" event happening is 1 minus the probability of the event occurring. For example, the probability of not rolling 6 three times in a row is $1 - \frac{1}{216} = \frac{215}{216}$.

Examples

1. **A deck of cards contains 40 cards divided into 4 colors: red, blue, green, and yellow. Each group has cards numbered 0–9. What is the probability of selecting an 8?**

   A. $\frac{1}{10}$ B. $\frac{1}{8}$ C. $\frac{1}{4}$ D. $\frac{1}{2}$

   The correct answer is **A**. The correct solution is $\frac{1}{10}$. There are 4 cards out of 40 that contain the number 8, making the probability $\frac{4}{40} = \frac{1}{10}$.

2. **A deck of cards contains 40 cards divided into 4 colors: red, blue, green, and yellow. Each group has cards numbered 0–9. What is the probability of selecting an even or a red card?**

   A. $\frac{1}{4}$ B. $\frac{3}{8}$ C. $\frac{5}{8}$ D. $\frac{3}{4}$

   The correct answer is **C**. The correct solution is $\frac{5}{8}$. There are 20 even cards and 10 red cards. The overlap of 5 red even cards is subtracted from the probability, $\frac{20}{40} + \frac{10}{40} - \frac{5}{40} = \frac{25}{40} = \frac{5}{8}$.

3. **A deck of cards contains 40 cards divided into 4 colors: red, blue, green, and yellow. Each group has cards numbered 0–9. What is the probability of selecting a blue card first, replacing the card, and selecting a 9?**

   A. $\frac{1}{100}$ B. $\frac{1}{80}$ C. $\frac{1}{40}$ D. $\frac{1}{20}$

   The correct answer is **C**. The correct solution is $\frac{1}{40}$. There are 10 blue cards and 4 cards that contain the number 9. The probability of the event is $\frac{10}{40} \times \frac{4}{40} = \frac{40}{1600} = \frac{1}{40}$.

4. **A deck of cards contains 40 cards divided into 4 colors: red, blue, green, and yellow. Each group has cards numbered 0–9. What is the probability of NOT selecting a green card?**

   A. $\frac{1}{4}$ B. $\frac{3}{8}$ C. $\frac{1}{2}$ D. $\frac{3}{4}$

   The correct answer is **D**. The correct solution is $\frac{3}{4}$. There are 10 cards that are green, making the probability of NOT selecting a green card $1 - \frac{10}{40} = \frac{30}{40} = \frac{3}{4}$.

Calculating Expected Values and Analyzing Decisions Based on Probability

The **expected value** of an event is the sum of the products of the probability of an event times the payoff of an event. A good example is calculating the expected value for buying a lottery ticket. There is a one in a hundred million chance that a person would win $50 million. Each ticket costs $2. The expected value is

$$\frac{1}{100,000,000}(50,000,000-2) + \frac{99,999,999}{100,000,000}(-2) = \frac{49,999,998}{100,000,000} - \frac{199,999,998}{100,000,000} = -\frac{150,000,000}{100,000,000} = -\$1.50$$

On average, one should expect to lose $1.50 each time the game is played. Analyzing the information, the meaning of the data shows that playing the lottery would result in losing money every time.

BE CAREFUL!

The expected value will not be the same as the actual value unless the probability of winning is 100%.

Examples

1. What is the expected value of an investment if the probability is $\frac{1}{5}$ of losing $1,000, $\frac{1}{4}$ of no gain, $\frac{2}{5}$ of making $1,000, and $\frac{3}{20}$ of making $2,000?

    A. $0

    B. $200

    C. $500

    D. $700

    The correct answer is **C**. The correct solution is $500. The expected value is $\frac{1}{5}(-1,000) + \frac{1}{4}(0) + \frac{2}{5}(1,000) + \frac{3}{20}(2,000) = -200 + 0 + 400 + 300 = \$500$.

2. The table below shows the value of the prizes and the probability of winning a prize in a contest.

Prize	$10	$100	$5,000	$50,000
Probability	1 in 50	1 in 1,000	1 in 50,000	1 in 250,000

    Calculate the expected value.

    A. $0.10

    B. $0.20

    C. $0.50

    D. $0.60

    The correct answer is **D**. The correct solution is $0.60. The probability for each event is

Prize	$10	$100	$5,000	$50,000	Not Winning
Probability	1 in 50 = 0.02	1 in 1,000 = 0.001	1 in 50,000 = 0.00002	1 in 250,000 = 0.000004	0.978976

    The expected value is $0.02(10) + 0.001(100) + 0.00002(5,000) + 0.000004(50,000) + 0.978976(0) =$

    $0.2 + 0.1 + 0.1 + 0.2 + 0 = \$0.60$.

3. **Which option results in the largest loss on a product?**

    A. 40% of gaining $100,000 and 60% of losing $100,000

    B. 60% of gaining $250,000 and 40% of losing $500,000

    C. 30% of gaining $400,000 and 70% of losing $250,000

    D. 60% of gaining $250,000 and 40% of losing $450,000

    The correct answer is **C**. The correct solution is 30% of gaining $400,000 and 70% of losing $250,000. The expected value is $0.30(400,000) + 0.7(-250,000) = 120,000 + (-175,000) = -55,000$.

Let's Review!

- The sample space is the number of outcomes of an event. The union, the intersection, and the complement are related to the sample space.
- The probability of an event is the number of possible events divided by the total number of outcomes. There can be "and," "or," and "not" probabilities.
- The expected value of an event is based on the payout and probability of an event occurring.

Interpreting Categorical and Quantitative Data

This lesson discusses how to represent and interpret data for a dot plot, a histogram, and a box plot. It compares multiple sets of data by using the measures of center and spread and examines the impact of outliers.

Representing Data on a Number Line

There are two types of data: quantitative and categorical. Quantitative variables are numerical, such as number of people in a household, bank account balance, and number of cars sold. Categorical variables are not numerical, and there is no inherent way to order them. Example are classes in college, types of pets, and party affiliations. The information for these data sets can be arranged on a number line using dot plots, histograms, and box plots.

A dot plot is a display of data using dots. The dots represent the number of times an item appears. Below is a sample of a dot plot.

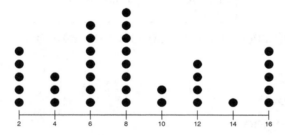

The mean and median can be determined by looking at a dot plot. The mean is the sum of all items divided by the number of dots. The median is the middle dot or the average of the middle two dots.

A histogram is a graphical display that has bars of various heights. It is similar to a bar chart, but the numbers are grouped into ranges. The bins, or ranges of values, of a histogram have equal lengths, such as 10 or 50 units. Continuous data such as weight, height, and amount of time are examples of data shown in a histogram. In the histogram to the right, the bin length is 8 units.

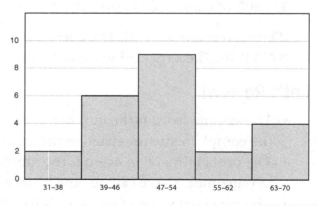

It is not possible to calculate the mean and median by looking at a histogram because there is a bin size rather than a single value on the horizontal axis. Histograms are beneficial when working with a large set of data.

BE CAREFUL!

Make sure to carefully interpret the data for any graphical display.

A box plot (or box-and-whisker plot) is a graphical display of the minimum, first quartile, median, third quartile, and maximum of a set of data. Recall the minimum is the smallest value and the maximum is the largest value in a set of data. The median is the middle number when the data set is written in order. The first quartile is the middle number between the minimum and the median. The third quartile is the middle number between the median and the maximum.

In the data display below, the minimum is 45, the first quartile is 50, the median is 57, the third quartile is 63, and the maximum is 75. With most box-and-whisker plots, the data is not symmetrical.

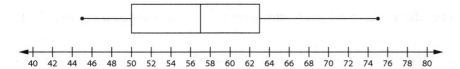

Example

The histogram below shows a basketball team's winning margin during the season. Which statement is true for the histogram?

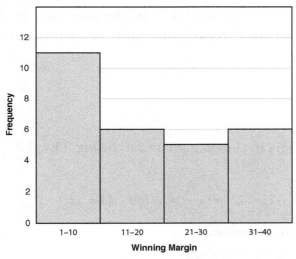

A. The team played a total of 30 games.

B. The frequency for 20–30 points is the same as for 30–40 points.

C. The sum of the frequency for the last two bins is the same as the first bin.

D. The frequency for 0–10 is twice the frequency for any other winning margin.

The correct answer is **C**. The correct solution is the sum of the frequency for the last two bins is the same as the first bin. The frequency of the first bin is 11, the frequency of the third bin is 5, and the frequency of the fourth bin is 6. The sum of the frequency of the last two bins is the same as the first bin.

Comparing Center and Spread of Multiple Data Sets

The measures of center are the mean (average) and median (middle number when written in order). These values describe the expected value of a data set. Very large or very small numbers affect the mean, but they do not affect the median.

The measures of spread are standard deviation (how far the numbers of a data set are from the mean) and interquartile range (the difference between the third and first quartile values).

To find the standard deviation:

- Find the mean.
- Find the difference between the mean and each member of the date set and square that result.
- Find the mean of the squared differences from the previous step.
- Apply the square root.

The larger the value for the standard deviation, the greater the spread of values from the mean. The larger the value for the interquartile range, the greater the spread of the middle 50% of values from the median.

Symmetric data has values that are close together, and the mean, median, and mode occur near the same value. The mean and standard deviation are used to explain multiple data sets and are evident in dot plots.

For example, consider this data set.

10, 10, 11, 11, 11, 12, 12, 12, 12, 12, 13, 13, 13, 14, 14

The mean is found by finding the sum of the numbers in the data set and dividing it by the number of items in the set, as follows:

$10 + 10 + 11 + 11 + 11 + 12 + 12 + 12 + 12 + 12 + 13 + 13 + 13 + 14 + 14 = 180 \div 15 = 12$.

The standard deviation calculation is shown in the table below.

Data	Data – Mean	(Data – Mean)^2
10	−2	4
10	−2	4
11	−1	1
11	−1	1
11	−1	1
12	0	0
12	0	0
12	0	0
12	0	0

Data	Data – Mean	(Data – Mean)²
12	0	0
13	1	1
13	1	1
13	1	1
14	2	4
14	2	4

The sum of the last column is 22. The standard deviation is $\sqrt{\frac{22}{15}} \approx 1.211$.

Next, consider this data set.

8, 8, 9, 10, 11, 12, 12, 12, 12, 12, 13, 14, 15, 16, 16

The mean is $8 + 8 + 9 + 10 + 11 + 12 + 12 + 12 + 12 + 12 + 13 + 14 + 15 + 16 + 16 = 180 \div 15 = 12$.

The standard deviation calculation is shown in the table below.

Data	Data – Mean	(Data – Mean)²
8	−4	16
8	−4	16
9	−3	9
10	−2	4
11	−1	1
12	0	0
12	0	0
12	0	0
12	0	0
12	0	0
13	1	1
14	2	4
15	3	9
16	4	16
16	4	16

The sum of the last column is 92. The standard deviation is $\sqrt{\frac{92}{15}} \approx 2.476$.

Therefore, the second set of data has values that are farther from the mean than the first data set.

When data is skewed, a group of its values are close and the remaining values are evenly spread. The median and interquartile range are used to explain multiple data sets and are evident in dot plots and box plots.

KEEP IN MIND

Compare the same measure of center or variation to draw accurate conclusions when comparing data sets.

The data set 10, 10, 11, 11, 11, 11, 11, 11, 12, 12, 12, 13, 13, 14, 15 has a median of 11 and an interquartile range of 2. The data set 10, 11, 12, 12, 13, 13, 14, 14, 14, 14, 14, 14, 14, 15, 15 has a median of 14 and an interquartile range of 2. The median is greater in the second data set, but the spread of data is the same for both sets of data.

Example

The box plots below show the heights of students in inches for two classes. Choose the statement that is true for the median and the interquartile range.

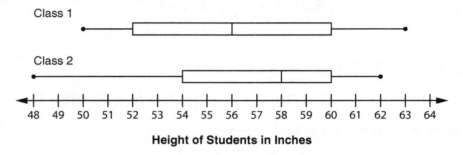

Height of Students in Inches

A. The median and interquartile range are greater for class 1.

B. The median and interquartile range are greater for class 2.

C. The median is greater for class 1, and the interquartile range is greater for class 2.

D. The median is greater for class 2, and the interquartile range is greater for class 1.

The correct answer is **D**. The correct solution is the median is greater for class 2, and the interquartile range is greater for class 1. The median is 58 inches for class 2 and 56 inches for class 1. The interquartile range is 8 inches for class 1 and 6 inches for class 2.

Determining the Effect of Extreme Data Points

An outlier is a value that is much smaller or much larger than rest of the values in a data set. This value has an impact on the mean and standard deviation values and occasionally has an impact on the median and interquartile range values.

The data set of 10, 10, 11, 11, 11, 12, 12, 12, 12, 12, 13, 13, 13, 14, 14 has a mean of 12 and a standard deviation of 1.211. If an outlier of 50 is added, the data set has a mean of has a mean of 14.38 and a standard deviation of 9.273. The outlier has

BE CAREFUL!
There may be a high outlier and a low outlier that may not have an impact on data.

increased the mean by more than 2, and the spread of the data has increased significantly.

The data set 10, 10, 11, 11, 11, 11, 11, 11, 12, 12, 12, 13, 13, 14, 15 has a median of 11 and an interquartile range of 2. If an outlier of 50 is added, the median slightly increases to 11.5 and the interquartile range remains 2.

Example

A little league basketball team scores 35, 38, 40, 36, 41, 42, 39, 35, 29, 32, 37, 33 in its first 12 games. In its next game, the team scores 12 points. Which statement describes the mean and standard deviation?

    A. The mean increases, and the standard deviation increases.

    B. The mean decreases, and the standard deviation increases.

    C. The mean increases, and the standard deviation decreases.

    D. The mean decreases, and the standard deviation decreases.

The correct answer is **B**. The correct solution is the mean decreases, and the standard deviation increases. The outlier value is lower than all other values, which results in a decrease for the mean. The standard deviation increases because the outlier of 12 is a value far away from the mean.

Let's Review!

- Dot plots, histograms, and box plots summarize and represent data on a number line.
- The mean and standard deviation are used to compare symmetric data sets.
- The median and interquartile range are used to compare skewed data sets.
- Outliers can impact measures of center and spread, particularly mean and standard deviation.

CHAPTER 9 STATISTICS AND PROBABILITY PRACTICE QUIZ

1. Two companies have made a chart of paid time off. Which statement describes the mean and standard deviation?

Paid Time off for Employees at Company A

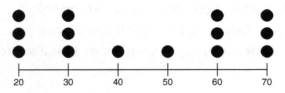

Paid Time off for Employees at Company B

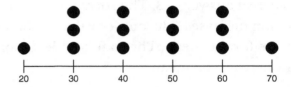

A. The means are the same, but the standard deviation is smaller for Company B.

B. The means are the same, but the standard deviation is smaller for Company A.

C. The mean is greater for Company A, and the standard deviation is smaller for Company A.

D. The mean is greater for Company B, and the standard deviation is smaller for Company B.

2. A basketball player scores 18, 17, 20, 23, 15, 24, 22, 28, 5. What is the effect of removing the outlier on the mean and standard deviation?

A. The mean and the standard deviation increase.

B. The mean and the standard deviation decrease.

C. The standard deviation increases, but the mean decreases.

D. The standard deviation decreases, but the mean increases.

3. Find the median from the dot plot.

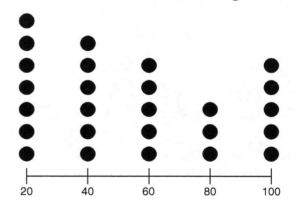

A. 40   C. 60

B. 50   D. 70

4. The table shows the number of students in grades kindergarten through sixth grade. Select the correct bar graph for this data.

Grade	Kindergarten	1st	2nd	3rd	4th	5th	6th
Number of Students	135	150	140	155	145	165	170

A.
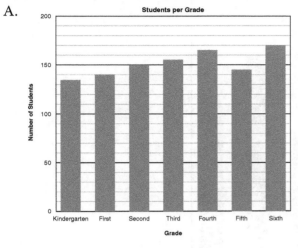

C.
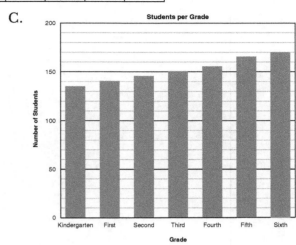

B.
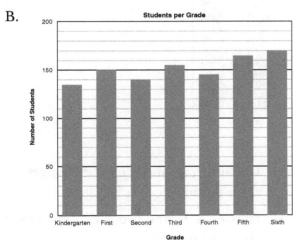

D.
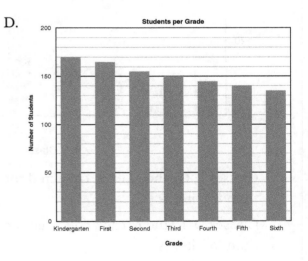

5. The bar chart shows the number of items collected for a charity drive. Which statement is true for the bar chart?

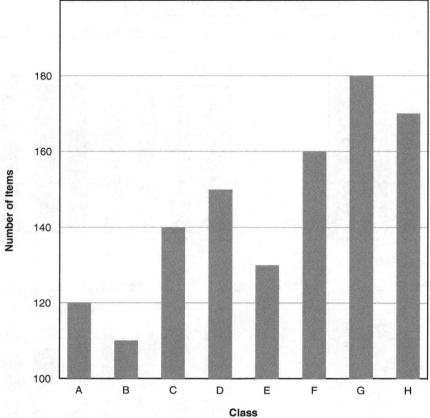

A. Classes F, G, and H each collected more than 150 items.

B. Classes D, F, and G each collected more than 150 items.

C. Classes C, D, and E each collected more than 140 items.

D. Classes A, B, and C each collected more than 140 items.

6. The circle graph shows the number of votes for each candidate. How many votes were cast for candidate D if there were 25,000 voters?

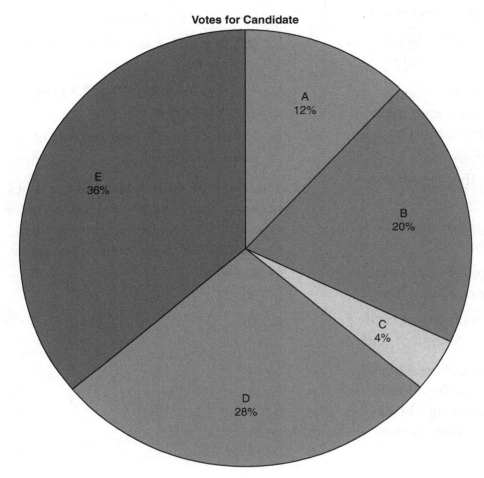

Votes for Candidate

A. 3,000 votes

B. 5,000 votes

C. 7,000 votes

D. 9,000 votes

7. A factory is investigating defects in screwdrivers that have been placed in containers to be shipped to stores. Random containers are selected for the team leader to review. What type of sampling is used?

A. Systematic sampling

B. Simple random sampling

C. Cluster random sampling

D. Stratified random sampling

8. A study looked at a random sample of people and watched their use of social media on mobile devices. The researcher looked at which group of users were happier. What type of study is this?

A. Census

B. Survey

C. Experiment

D. Observational study

9. There are four available pen colors to choose. A simulation is used to represent the number of times each pen is used.

Red	Blue	Black	Green	Total
1,248	1,260	1,247	1,245	5,000

Choose the statement that correctly explains why or why not seeing these results questions the probability of one out of four for each color.

A. Yes, because of the limited number of outcomes

B. Yes, because not enough simulations were completed

C. No, because the probability of each color is not exactly one out of four

D. No, because the probability of each color is very close to one out of four

10. A bag contains 10 red marbles, 8 black marbles, and 7 white marbles. What is the probability of selecting a black marble first and a red marble second with no replacement?

A. $\frac{8}{25}$

B. $\frac{16}{125}$

C. $\frac{2}{15}$

D. $\frac{7}{75}$

11. Which option results in the greatest gain on an investment?

A. 100% of gaining $1,000

B. 60% of gaining $2,500 and 40% of gaining $0

C. 75% of gaining $1,000 and 25% of gaining $1,500

D. 70% of gaining $1,500 and 30% of gaining $1,000

12. There are 60 students attending classes in town. There are 40 students in dance class and 30 students in art class. Find the number of students in either dance or art class.

A. 30

B. 40

C. 50

D. 60

CHAPTER 9 STATISTICS AND PROBABILITY PRACTICE QUIZ – ANSWER KEY

1. A. The correct solution is the means are the same, but the standard deviation is smaller for Company B. The standard deviation is smaller for Company B because more values are closer to the mean. **See Lesson: Interpreting Categorical and Quantitative Data.**

2. D. The correct solution is the standard deviation decreases, but the mean increases. The standard deviation from 6.226 and 3.951 when the low outlier is removed. The mean increases from 19.11 to 20.88 because the outlier, 5, is the lowest value. **See Lesson: Interpreting Categorical and Quantitative Data.**

3. B. The correct solution is 50. The middle two values are 40 and 60, and the average of these values is 50. **See Lesson: Interpreting Categorical and Quantitative Data.**

4. B. The correct solution is B because the number of students for each grade is correct. **See Lesson: Interpreting Graphics.**

5. A. The correct solution is classes F, G, and H collected more than 150 items. Class F collected 160 items, class G collected 180 items, and class H collected 170 items. **See Lesson: Interpreting Graphics.**

6. C. The correct solution is 7,000 votes because 28% of 25,000 is 7,000 voters. **See Lesson: Interpreting Graphics.**

7. D. The correct solution is stratified random sampling because the screwdrivers are placed into containers and the containers are randomly selected. **See Lesson: Statistical Measures.**

8. D. The correct solution is observational study because people were not randomly assigned to group and their behaviors were observed. **See Lesson: Statistical Measures.**

9. D. The correct solution is no, because the probability of each color is very close to one out of four. The more simulations, the closer the results will be to the actual probability of one out of four for each color. **See Lesson: Statistical Measures.**

10. C. The correct solution is $\frac{2}{15}$. There are 8 marbles out of 25 for the first event and 10 marbles out of 24 for the second event. The probability of the event is $\frac{8}{25} \times \frac{10}{24} = \frac{80}{600} = \frac{2}{15}$. **See Lesson: Statistics & Probability: The Rules of Probability.**

11. B. The correct solution is 60% of gaining $2,500 and 40% of gaining $0. The expected value is $0.60(2,500) + 0.40(0) = \$1,500$. **See Lesson: Statistics & Probability: The Rules of Probability.**

12. C. The correct solution 50 because there are 70 students in both classes less the total students is 10 students. Then, subtract 10 students from the total, which is 50 students. **See Lesson: Statistics & Probability: The Rules of Probability.**

SECTION III. READING

CHAPTER 10 KEY IDEAS AND DETAILS

MAIN IDEAS, TOPIC SENTENCES, AND SUPPORTING DETAILS

To read effectively, you need to know how to identify the most important information in a text. You must also understand how ideas within a text relate to one other.

Main Ideas

The central or most important idea in a text is the **main idea**. As a reader, you need to avoid confusing the main idea with less important details that may be interesting but not central to the author's point.

The **topic** of a text is slightly different than the main idea. The topic is a word or phrase that describes roughly what a text is about. A main idea, in contrast, is a complete sentence that states the topic and explains what an author wants to say about it.

All types of texts can contain main ideas. Read the following informational paragraph and try to identify the main idea:

> The immune system is the body's defense mechanism. It fights off harmful bacteria, viruses, and substances that attack the body. To do this, it uses cells, tissues, and organs that work together to resist invasion.

The topic of this paragraph is the immune system. The main idea can be expressed in a sentence like this: "This paragraph defines and describes the immune system." Ideas about organisms and substances that invade the body are not the central focus. The topic and main idea must always be directly related to every sentence in the text, as the immune system is here.

Read the persuasive paragraph below and consider the topic and main idea:

> Football is not a healthy activity for kids. It causes head injuries that harm the ability to learn and achieve. It causes painful bodily injuries that can linger into adulthood. It teaches aggressive behavioral habits that make life harder for players after they have left the field.

The topic of this paragraph is youth football, and the main idea is that kids should not play the game. Note that if you are asked to state the main idea of a persuasive text, it is your job to be objective. This means you should describe the author's opinion, not make an argument of your own in response.

Both of the example paragraphs above state their main idea explicitly. Some texts have an implicit, or suggested, main idea. In this case, you need to figure out the main idea using the details as clues.

FOR EXAMPLE

The following fictional paragraph has an implicit main idea:

Daisy parked her car and sat gripping the wheel, not getting out. A few steps to the door. A couple of knocks. She could give him the news in two words. She'd already decided what she was going to do, so it didn't matter what he said, not really. Still, she couldn't make her feet carry her to the door.

The main idea here is that Daisy feels reluctant to speak to someone. This point is not stated outright, but it is clear from the details of Daisy's thoughts and actions.

Topic Sentences

Many paragraphs identify the topic and main idea in a single sentence. This is called a **topic sentence**, and it often appears at the beginning of a paragraph. However, a writer may choose to place a topic sentence anywhere in the text.

Some paragraphs contain an introductory sentence to grab the reader's attention before clearly stating the topic. A paragraph may begin by asking a rhetorical question, presenting a striking idea, or showing why the topic is important. When authors use this strategy, the topic sentence usually comes second:

> Have you ever wondered how your body fights off a nasty cold? **It uses a complex defense mechanism called the immune system.** The immune system fights off harmful bacteria, viruses, and substances that attack the body. To do this, it uses cells, tissues, and organs that work together to resist invasion.

Here, the first sentence grabs the attention, and the second, **boldfaced** topic sentence states the main idea. The remaining sentences provide further information, explaining what the immune system does and identifying its basic components.

COMPARE!

The informational paragraph above contains a question that grabs the attention at the beginning. The writer could convey the same information with a little less flair by omitting this device. The version you read in Section 1 does exactly this. (The topic sentence below is **boldfaced**.)

The immune system is the body's defense mechanism. It fights off harmful bacteria, viruses, and substances that attack the body. To do this, it uses cells, tissues, and organs that work together to resist invasion.

Look back at the football paragraph from Section 1. Which sentence is the topic sentence?

Sometimes writers wait until the end of a paragraph to reveal the main idea in a topic sentence. When you're reading a paragraph that is organized this way, you may feel like you're reading a bit of a puzzle. It's not fully clear what the piece is about until you get to the end:

> It causes head injuries that harm the ability to learn and achieve. It causes painful bodily injuries that can linger through the passage of years. It teaches aggressive behavioral habits that make life harder for players after they have left the field. **Football is not a healthy activity for kids.**

Note that the topic—football—is not actually named until the final, **boldfaced** topic sentence. This is a strong hint that this final sentence is the topic sentence. Other paragraphs with this structure may contain several examples or related ideas and then tie them together with a summary statement near the end.

Supporting Details

The **supporting details** of a text develop the main idea, contribute further information, or provide examples.

All of the supporting details in a text must relate back to the main idea. In a text that sets out to define and describe the immune system, the supporting details could explain how the immune system works, define parts of the immune system, and so on.

> **Main Idea:** The immune system is the body's defense mechanism.
>
> **Supporting Detail:** It fights off harmful bacteria, viruses, and substances that attack the body.
>
> **Supporting Detail:** To do this, it uses cells, tissues, and organs that work together to resist invasion.

The above text could go on to describe white blood cells, which are a vital part of the body's defense system against disease. However, the supporting details in such a text should *not* drift off into descriptions of parts of the body that make no contribution to immune response.

Supporting details may be facts or opinions. A single text can combine both facts and opinions to develop a single main idea.

> **Main Idea:** Football is not a healthy activity for kids.
>
> **Supporting Detail:** It teaches aggressive behavioral habits that make life harder for players after they have left the field.
>
> **Supporting Detail:** In a study of teenage football players by Dr. Sophia Ortega at Harvard University, 28% reported involvement in fights or other violent incidents, compared with 19% of teenage boys who were not involved in sports.

The first supporting detail above states an opinion. The second is still related to the main idea, but it provides factual information to back up the opinion. Further development of this paragraph could contain other types of facts, including information about football injuries and anecdotes about real players who got hurt playing the game.

Let's Review!

- The main idea is the most important piece of information in a text.
- The main idea is often expressed in a topic sentence.
- Supporting details develop the main idea, contribute further information, or provide examples.

SUMMARIZING TEXT AND USING TEXT FEATURES

Effective readers need to know how to identify and restate the main idea of a text through summary. They must also follow complex instructions, figure out the sequence of events in a text that is not presented in order, and understand information presented in graphics.

Summary Basics

A **summary** is a text that restates the ideas from a different text in a new way. Every summary needs to include the main idea of the original. Some summaries may include information about the supporting details as well.

The content and level of detail in a summary vary depending on the purpose. For example, a journalist may summarize a recent scientific study in a newspaper profile of its authors. A graduate student might briefly summarize the same study in a paper questioning its conclusions. The journalist's version would likely use fairly simple language and restate only the main points. The student's version would likely use specialized scientific vocabulary and include certain supporting details, especially the ones most applicable to the argument the student intends to make later.

The language of a summary must be substantially different from the original. It should not retain the structure and word choice of the source text. Rather, it should provide a completely new way of stating the ideas.

Read the passage below and the short summary that follows:

> **Original:** There is no need for government regulations to maintain a minimum wage because free market forces naturally adjust wages on their own. Workers are in short supply in our thriving economy, and businesses must offer fair wages and working conditions to attract labor. Business owners pay employees well because common sense dictates that they cannot succeed any other way.

> **Effective Summary:** The author argues against minimum wage laws. He claims free market forces naturally keep wages high in a healthy economy with a limited labor supply.

KEY POINT!

Many ineffective summaries attempt to imitate the structure of the original text and change only individual words. This makes the writing process difficult, and it can lead to unintentional plagiarism.

Ineffective Summary (Plagiarism): It is unnecessary for government regulations to create a minimum wage because capitalism adjusts wages without help. Good labor is rare in our excellent economy, and businesses need to offer fair wages and working conditions in order to attract workers.

The above text is an example of structural plagiarism. Summary writing does not just involve rewriting the original words one by one. An effective summary restates the main ideas of the text in a wholly original way.

Study the infographic below and answer questions 7-9.

https://www.cdc.gov/nccdphp/dch/images/infographics/getmoving_15-18.png

Credit: Center for Disease Control and Prevention. https://www.cdc.gov/nccdphp/dnpao/multimedia/infographics/getmoving.html

7. Which of the following is not a sign that the infographic is credible?

    A. The use of verifiable facts

    B. The list of source materials

    C. The professional appearance

    D. The inclusion of an author's name

8. Zetta is unsure of the credibility of this source and has never heard of the Centers for Disease Control (CDC). Which fact could help her decide to trust it?

    A. The CDC is located in Atlanta.

    B. The CDC has a .gov web address.

    C. The CDC creates many infographics.

    D. The CDC is also listed as a source consulted.

9. What could a skeptical reader do to verify the facts on the infographic?

    A. Interview one teenager to ask about his or her screen time.

    B. Follow the links for the sources and determine their credibility.

    C. Check a tertiary source like Wikipedia to verify the information.

    D. Find different values for screen time on someone's personal blog.

CHAPTER 10 KEY IDEAS AND DETAILS PRACTICE QUIZ – ANSWER KEY

1. A. A diagram illustrates complex visual ideas, so it could show which part of a bicycle is which and how they fit together. **See Lesson: Summarizing Text and Using Text Features.**

2. B. The sentence above conveys factual information about Mars in an excited tone that suggests a positive interest in the subject. This makes it most likely to fit into an informational paragraph sharing facts about Mars. **See Lesson: Main Ideas, Topic Sentences, and Supporting Details.**

3. D. If the above sentence were a topic sentence, its supporting details would likely share information to develop the idea that Mars may have supported life in the past. **See Lesson: Main Ideas, Topic Sentences, and Supporting Details.**

4. C. The sentence above could act as an example to show how space discoveries teach us about Earth and ourselves. **See Lesson: Main Ideas, Topic Sentences, and Supporting Details.**

5. C. Larger bars in a bar graph indicate higher numbers. This book has sold more paperback copies than any other. **See Lesson: Summarizing Text and Using Text Features.**

6. B. The bar graph shows fewer hardcover sales than any other kind. This could help support an argument that later books should only be released in electronic and paperback forms. **See Lesson: Summarizing Text and Using Text Features.**

7. D. It is usually a good sign if an author is clearly named in a source. Although this source is authored by an organization, the CDC, instead of a single author, there are many other signs it is credible. **See Lesson: Understanding Primary Sources, Making Inferences, and Drawing Conclusions.**

8. B. When presenting this type of information, a government organization with a .gov web address is typically considered a reputable source. **See Lesson: Understanding Primary Sources, Making Inferences, and Drawing Conclusions.**

9. B. One way to verify facts is to check the sources an author used. Verifying facts elsewhere may also be a good idea, but it is important to use reputable primary or secondary sources. **See Lesson: Understanding Primary Sources, Making Inferences, and Drawing Conclusions.**

CHAPTER 11 CRAFT AND STRUCTURE

FORMAL AND INFORMAL LANGUAGE

In English, there is formal language that is used most often in writing, and informal language that is most often used in speaking, but there are situations where one is more appropriate than the other. This lesson will cover differentiating contexts for (1) formal language and (2) informal language.

Formal Language

Formal language is often associated with writing for professional and academic purposes, but it is also used when giving a speech or a lecture. An essay written for a class will always use **formal language**. **Formal language** is used in situations where people are not extremely close and when one needs to show respect to another person. Certain qualities and contexts differentiate **formal language** from informal language.

Formal language does not use contractions.

- It doesn't have that - It does not have that.
- He's been offered a new job - He has been offered a new job.

Formal language also uses complete sentences.

- So much to tell you - I have so much to tell you.
- Left for the weekend - We left for the weekend.

Formal language includes more formal and polite vocabulary.

- The class starts at two - The class commences at two.
- I try to be the best person I can be - I endeavor to be the best person I can be.

Formal language is not personal and normally does not use the pronouns "I" and "We" as the subject of a sentence.

- I argue that the sky is blue - This essay argues that the sky is blue.
- We often associate green with grass - Green is often associated with grass.

Formal language also does not use slang.

- It's raining cats and dogs - It is raining heavily.
- Patients count on doctors to help them - Patients expect doctors to help them.

Informal Language

Informal language is associated with speaking, but is also used in text messages, emails, letters, and postcards. It is the language a person would use with their friends and family.

Informal language uses contractions.

- I can't go to the movie tomorrow.
- He doesn't have any manners.

Informal language can include sentence fragments.

- See you
- Talk to you later

Informal language uses less formal vocabulary such as slang.

- The dog drove me up the wall.
- I was so hungry I could eat a horse.
- I can always count on you.

Informal language is personal and uses pronouns such as "I" and "We" as the subject of a sentence.

- I am in high school.
- We enjoy going to the beach in the summer.

Let's Review!

- **Formal language** is used in professional and academic writing and talks. It does not have contractions, uses complete sentences, uses polite and formal vocabulary, not slang, and is not personal and generally does not use the pronouns "I" and "We" as the subject of a sentence.
- **Informal language** is used in daily life when communicating with friends and family through conversations, text messages, emails, letters, and postcards. It uses contractions, can be sentence fragments, uses less formal vocabulary and slang, and is personal and uses pronouns such as "I" and "We" as the subject of a sentence.

TONE, MOOD, AND TRANSITION WORDS

Authors use language to show their emotions and to make readers feel something too. They also use transition words to help guide the reader from one idea to the next.

Tone and Mood

The **tone** of a text is the author's or speaker's attitude toward the subject. The tone may reflect any feeling or attitude a person can express: happiness, excitement, anger, boredom, or arrogance.

Readers can identify tone primarily by analyzing word choice. The reader should be able to point to specific words and details that help to establish the tone.

> **Example:** The train rolled past miles and miles of cornfields. The fields all looked the same. They swayed the same. They produced the same dull nausea in the pit of my stomach. I'd been sent out to see the world, and so I looked, obediently. What I saw was sameness.

Here, the author is expressing boredom and dissatisfaction. This is clear from the repetition of words like "same" and "sameness." There's also a sense of unpleasantness from phrases like "dull nausea" and passivity from words like "obediently."

Sometimes an author uses an ironic tone. Ironic texts often mean the opposite of what they actually say. To identify irony, you need to rely on your prior experience and common sense to help you identify texts with words and ideas that do not quite match.

> **Example:** With that, the senator dismissed the petty little problem of mass shootings and returned to the really important issue: his approval ratings.

BE CAREFUL!

When you're asked to identify the tone of a text, be sure to keep track of *whose* tone you're supposed to identify, and which part of the text the question is referencing. The author's tone can be different from that of the characters in fiction or the people quoted in nonfiction.

Example: The reporter walked quickly, panting to catch up to the senator's entourage. "Senator Biltong," she said. "Are you going to take action on mass shootings?"

"Sure, sure. Soon," the senator said vaguely. Then he turned to greet a newcomer. "Ah ha! Here's the man who can fix my approval ratings!" And with that, he returned to the really important issue: his popularity.

*

In the example above, the author's tone is ironic and angry. But the tone of the senator's dialogue is different. The line beginning with the words "Sure, sure" has a distracted tone. The line beginning with "Ah ha!" has a pleased tone.

Here the author flips around the words most people would usually use to discuss mass murder and popularity. By calling a horrific issue "petty" and a trivial issue "important," the author highlights what she sees as a politician's backwards priorities. Except for the phrase "mass shootings," the words here are light and airy—but the tone is ironic and angry.

A concept related to tone is **mood**, or the feelings an author produces in the reader. To determine the mood of a text, a reader can consider setting and theme as well as word choice and tone. For example, a story set in a haunted house may produce an unsettled or frightened feeling in a reader.

Tone and mood are often confused. This is because they are sometimes the same. For instance, in an op-ed article that describes children starving while food aid lies rotting, the author may use an outraged tone and simultaneously arouse an outraged mood in the reader.

However, tone and mood can be different. When they are, it's useful to have different words to distinguish between the author's attitude and the reader's emotional reaction.

> **Example:** I had to fly out of town at 4 a.m. for my trip to the Bahamas, and my wife didn't even get out of bed to make me a cup of coffee. I told her to, but she refused just because she'd been up five times with our newborn. I'm only going on vacation for one week, and she's been off work for a month! She should show me a little consideration.

Here, the tone is indignant. The mood will vary depending on the reader, but it is likely to be unsympathetic.

Transitions

Authors use connecting words and phrases, or **transitions**, to link ideas and help readers follow the flow of their thoughts. The number of possible ways to transition between ideas is almost limitless.

Below are a few common transition words, categorized by the way they link ideas.

Transitions	Examples
Time and sequence transitions orient the reader within a text. They can also help show when events happened in time.	*First, second, next, now, then, at this point, after, afterward, before this, previously, formerly, thereafter, finally, in conclusion*
Addition or emphasis transitions let readers know the author is building on an established line of thought. Many place extra stress on an important idea.	*Moreover, also, likewise, furthermore, above all, indeed, in fact*
Example transitions introduce ideas that illustrate a point.	*For example, for instance, to illustrate, to demonstrate*
Causation transitions indicate a cause-and-effect relationship.	*As a result, consequently, thus*
Contrast transitions indicate a difference between ideas.	*Nevertheless, despite, in contrast, however*

Transitions may look different depending on their function within the text. Within a paragraph, writers often choose short words or expressions to provide transitions and smooth the flow. Between paragraphs or larger sections of text, transitions are usually longer. They may use some of the key words or ideas above, but the author often goes into detail restating larger concepts and explaining their relationships more thoroughly.

Between Sentences: Students who cheat do not learn what they need to know. *As a result,* they get farther behind and face greater temptation to cheat in the future.

Between Paragraphs: *As a result of the cheating behaviors described above,* students find themselves in a vicious cycle.

Longer transitions like the latter example may be useful for keeping the reader clued in to the author's focus in an extended text. But long transitions should have clear content and function. Some long transitions, such as the very wordy "due to the fact that" take up space without adding more meaning and are considered poor style.

Let's Review!

- Tone is the author's or speaker's attitude toward the subject.
- Mood is the feeling a text creates in the reader.
- Transitions are connecting words and phrases that help readers follow the flow of a writer's thoughts.

THE AUTHOR'S PURPOSE AND POINT OF VIEW

In order to understand, analyze, and evaluate a text, readers must know how to identify the author's purpose and point of view. Readers also need to attend to an author's language and rhetorical strategies.

Author's Purpose

When writers put words on paper, they do it for a reason. This reason is the author's **purpose**. Most writing exists for one of three purposes: to inform, to persuade, or to entertain.

TEST TIP

You may have learned about a fourth purpose for writing: conveying an emotional experience. Many poems as well as some works of fiction, personal essays, and memoirs are written to give the reader a sense of how an event or moment might feel. This type of text is rarely included on placement tests, and if it is, it tends to be lumped in with literature meant to entertain.

If a text is designed to share knowledge, its purpose is to **inform**. Informational texts include technical documents, cookbooks, expository essays, journalistic newspaper articles, and many nonfiction books. Informational texts are based on facts and logic, and they usually attempt an objective tone. The style may otherwise vary; some informational texts are quite dry, whereas others have an engaging style.

If a text argues a point, its purpose is to **persuade**. A persuasive text attempts to convince a reader to believe a certain point of view or take a certain action. Persuasive texts include op-ed newspaper articles, book and movie reviews, project proposals, and argumentative essays. Key signs of persuasive texts include judgments, words like *should,* and other signs that the author is sharing opinions.

If a text is primarily for fun, its purpose is to **entertain**. Entertaining texts usually tell stories or present descriptions. Entertaining texts include novels, short stories, memoirs, and some poems. Virtually all stories are lumped into this category, even if they describe unpleasant experiences.

CONNECTIONS

You may have read elsewhere that readers can break writing down into the following basic categories. These categories are often linked to the author's purpose.

Narrative writing tells a story and is usually meant to entertain.
Expository writing explains an idea and is usually meant to inform.
Technical writing explains a mechanism or process and is usually meant to inform.
Persuasive writing argues a point and, as the label suggests, is meant to persuade.

A text can have more than one purpose. For example, many traditional children's stories come with morals or lessons. These are meant both to entertain children and persuade them to behave in ways society considers appropriate. Also, commercial nonfiction texts like popular science books are often written in an engaging or humorous style. The purpose of such a text is to inform while also entertaining the reader.

Point of View

Every author has a general outlook or set of opinions about the subject. These make up the author's **point of view**.

To determine point of view, a reader must recognize implicit clues in the text and use them to develop educated guesses about the author's worldview. In persuasive texts, the biggest clue is the author's explicit argument. From considering this argument, a reader can usually make some inferences about point of view. For instance, if an author argues that parents should offer kids opportunities to exercise throughout the day, it would be reasonable to infer that the author has an overall interest in children's health, and that he or she is troubled by the idea of kids pursuing sedentary behaviors like TV watching.

It is more challenging to determine point of view in a text meant to inform. Because the writer does not present an explicit argument, readers must examine assumptions and word choice to determine the writer's point of view.

> **Example:** Models suggest that at the current rate of global warming, hurricanes in 2100 will move 9 percent slower and drop 24 percent more rain. Longer storm durations and rainfall rates will likely translate to increased economic damage and human suffering.

It is reasonable to infer that the writer of this passage has a general trust for science and scientists. This writer assumes that global warming is happening, so it is clear he or she is not a global warming denier. Although the writer does not suggest a plan to prevent future storm damage, the emphasis on negative effects and the use of negative words like "damage" and "suffering" suggest that the author is worried about global warming.

Texts meant to entertain also contain clues about the author's point of view. That point of view is usually evident from the themes and deeper meanings. For instance, a memoirist who writes an upbeat story about a troubled but loving family is likely to believe strongly in the power of love. Note, however, that in this type of work, it is not possible to determine point of view merely from one character's words or actions. For instance, if a character says, "Your mother's love doesn't matter much if she can't take care of you," the reader should *not* automatically assume the writer agrees with that statement. Narrative writers often present a wide range of characters with varying outlooks on life. A reader can only determine the author's point of view by considering the work as a whole. The attitudes that are most emphasized and the ones that win out in the end are likely to reflect the author's point of view.

Rhetorical Strategies

Rhetorical strategies are the techniques an author uses to support an argument or develop a main idea. Effective readers need to study the language of a text and determine how the author is supporting his or her points.

One strategy is to appeal to the reader's reason. This is the foundation of effective writing, and it simply means that the writer relies on factual information and the logical conclusions that follow from it. Even persuasive writing uses this strategy by presenting facts and reasons to back up the author's opinions.

> **Ineffective:** Everyone knows *Sandra and the Lumps* is the best band of the new millennium.

> **Effective:** The three most recent albums by *Sandra and the Lumps* are the first, second, and third most popular records released since the turn of the millennium.

Another strategy is to establish trust. A writer can do this by choosing credible sources and by presenting ideas in a clear and professional way. In persuasive writing, writers may show they are trustworthy by openly acknowledging that some people hold contradicting opinions and by responding fairly to those positions. Writers should never attack or misrepresent their opponents' position.

> **Ineffective:** People who refuse to recycle are too lazy to protect their children's future.

> **Effective:** According to the annual Throw It Out Questionnaire, many people dislike the onerous task of sorting garbage, and some doubt that their effort brings any real gain.

A final strategy is to appeal to the reader's emotions. For instance, a journalist reporting on the opioid epidemic could include a personal story about an addict's attempts to overcome substance abuse. Emotional content can add a human dimension to a story that would be missing if the writer only included statistics and expert opinions. But emotions are easily manipulated, so writers who use this strategy need to be careful. Emotions should never be used to distort the truth or scare readers into agreeing with the writer.

> **Ineffective:** If you don't take action on gun control, you're basically killing children.

> **Effective:** Julie was puzzling over the Pythagorean Theorem when she heard the first gunshot.

Let's Review!

- Every text has a purpose.
- Most texts are meant to inform, persuade, or entertain.
- Texts contain clues that imply an author's outlook or set of opinions about the subject.
- Authors use rhetorical strategies to appeal to reason, establish trust, or invoke emotions.

Chapter 11 Craft and Structure Practice Quiz

1. **Which of the following sentences uses the MOST informal language?**

   A. The house creaked at night.

   B. I ate dinner with my friend.

   C. It's sort of a bad time.

   D. The water trickled slowly.

2. **In which of the following situations would it be best to use informal language?**

   A. In a seminar

   B. Writing a postcard

   C. Talking to your boss

   D. Participating in a professional conference

3. **Which of the following sentences uses the MOST formal language?**

   A. Thanks for letting me know.

   B. I want to thank you for telling me.

   C. I appreciate you telling me about this issue.

   D. Thank you for bringing this issue to my attention.

Read the passage below and answer questions 4-6.

The train was the most amazing thing ever even though it didn't go "choo choo." The toddler pounded on the railing of the bridge and supplied the sound herself. "Choo choo! Choo choooooo!" she shouted as the train cars whizzed along below.

In the excitement, she dropped her favorite binky.

Later, when she noticed the binky missing, all the joy went out of the world. The wailing could be heard three houses down. The toddler's usual favorite activities were garbage—even waving to Hank the garbage man, which she refused to do, so that Hank went away looking mildly hurt. It was clear the little girl would never, ever, ever recover from her loss.

Afterward, she played at the park.

4. **Which adjectives best describe the tone of the passage?**

   A. Ironic, angry

   B. Earnest, angry

   C. Ironic, humorous

   D. Earnest, humorous

5. **Which sentence from the passage is clearly ironic?**

   A. "Choo choo! Choo choooooo!" she shouted as the train cars whizzed along below.

   B. Later, when she noticed the binky missing, all the joy went out of the world.

   C. The wailing could be heard three houses down.

   D. Afterward, she played at the park.

6. The author of the passage first establishes the ironic tone by:

   A. describing the child's trip to play at the park.

   B. calling the train "the most amazing thing ever."

   C. pretending that the child can make the sounds "choo chooooo!"

   D. claiming inaccurately that the lost binky was the child's "favorite."

7. What is the most likely purpose of a popular science book describing recent advances in genetics?

   A. To decide   C. To persuade

   B. To inform   D. To entertain

8. Which phrase describes the set of techniques an author uses to support an argument or develop a main idea?

   A. Points of view

   B. Logical fallacies

   C. Statistical analyses

   D. Rhetorical strategies

9. What is the most likely purpose of an article that claims some genetic research is immoral?

   A. To decide   C. To persuade

   B. To inform   D. To entertain

CHAPTER 11 CRAFT AND STRUCTURE PRACTICE QUIZ – ANSWER KEY

1. C. *It's sort of a bad time.* The sentence has contractions and uses informal and slang words. **See Lesson: Formal and Informal Language.**

2. B. *Writing a postcard.* It is an informal mode of communication between close friends and relatives. **See Lesson: Formal and Informal Language.**

3. D. *Thank you for bringing this issue to my attention.* The sentence uses the most formal and polite vocabulary. **See Lesson: Formal and Informal Language.**

4. C. This passage ironically is a humorous description of a toddler's emotions, written by an adult who has enough experience to know that a toddler's huge emotions will pass. **See Lesson: Tone, Mood, and Transition Words.**

5. B. Authors use irony when their words do not literally mean what they say. The joy does not really go out of the world when a toddler loses her binky—but it may seem that way to the child. **See Lesson: Tone, Mood, and Transition Words.**

6. B. This passage establishes irony in the opening sentence by applying the superlative phrase "the most amazing thing ever" to an ordinary occurrence. **See Lesson: Tone, Mood, and Transition Words.**

7. B. If a book is describing information, its purpose is to inform. **See Lesson: The Author's Purpose and Point of View.**

8. D. The techniques an author uses to support an argument or develop a main idea are called rhetorical strategies. **See Lesson: The Author's Purpose and Point of View.**

9. C. An article that takes a moral position is meant to persuade. **See Lesson: The Author's Purpose and Point of View.**

Chapter 12 Integration of Knowledge and Ideas

Facts, Opinions, and Evaluating an Argument

Nonfiction writing is based on facts and real events, but most nonfiction nevertheless expresses a point of view. Effective readers must evaluate the author's point of view and form their own conclusions about the points in the text.

Fact and Opinion

Many texts make an **argument.** In this context, the word *argument* has nothing to do with anger or fighting. It simply means the author is trying to convince readers of something.

Arguments are present in a wide variety of texts. Some relate to controversial issues, for instance by advocating support for a political candidate or change in laws. Others may defend a certain interpretation of facts or ideas. For example, a literature paper may argue that an author's story suggests a certain theme, or a science paper may argue for a certain interpretation of data. An argument may also present a plan of action such as a business strategy.

To evaluate an argument, readers must distinguish between **fact** and **opinion.** A fact is verifiably true. An opinion is someone's belief.

> **Fact:** Seattle gets an average of 37 inches of rain per year.

> **Opinion:** The dark, rainy, cloudy weather makes Seattle an unpleasant place to live in winter.

Meteorologists measure rainfall directly, so the above fact is verifiably true. The statement "it is unpleasant" clearly reflects a feeling, so the second sentence is an opinion.

The difference between fact and opinion is not always straightforward. For instance, a text may present a fact that contains an opinion within it:

> **Fact:** Nutritionist Fatima Antar questions the wisdom of extreme carbohydrate avoidance.

Assuming the writer can prove that this sentence genuinely reflects Fatima Antar's beliefs, it is a factual statement of her point of view. The reader may trust that Fatima Antar really holds this opinion, whether or not the reader is convinced by it.

If a text makes a judgment, it is not a fact:

Opinion: The patient's seizure drug regimen caused horrendous side effects.

This sentence uses language that different people would interpret in different ways. Because people have varying ideas about what they consider "horrendous," this sentence is an opinion as it is written, even though the actual side effects and the patient's opinion of them could both be verified.

COMPARE!

Small changes to the statement about seizure drugs could turn it into a factual statement:

Fact: The patient's seizure drug regiment caused side effects such as migraines, confusion, and dangerously high blood pressure.

The above statement can be verified because the patient and other witnesses could confirm the exact nature of her symptoms. This makes it a fact.

Fact: The patient reported that her seizure drug regimen caused horrendous side effects.

This statement can also be verified because the patient can verify that she considers the side effects horrendous. By framing the statement in this way, the writer leaves nothing up to interpretation and is clearly in the realm of fact.

The majority of all arguments contain both facts and opinions, and strong arguments may contain both fact and opinion elements. It is rare for an argument to be composed entirely of facts, but it can happen if the writer is attempting to convince readers to accept factual information that is little-known or widely questioned. Most arguments present an author's opinion and use facts, reasoning, and expert testimony to convince readers.

Evaluating an Argument

Effective readers must evaluate an argument and decide whether or not it is valid. To do this, readers must consider every claim the author presents, including both the main argument and any supporting statements. If an argument is based on poor reasoning or insufficient evidence, it is not valid—even if you agree with the main idea.

KEY POINT!

Most of us want to agree with arguments that reflect our own beliefs. But it is inadvisable to accept an argument that is not properly rooted in good reasoning. Consider the following statements about global climate change:

Poor Argument: It just snowed fifteen inches! How can anyone say the world is getting warmer?

Poor Argument: It's seventy degrees in the middle of February! How can anyone deny global warming?

Both of these arguments are based on insufficient evidence. Each relies on *one* weather event in *one* location to support an argument that the entire world's climate is or is not changing. There is not nearly enough information here to support an argument on either side.

Beware of any argument that presents opinion information as fact.

False Claim of Fact: I know vaccines cause autism because my niece began displaying autism symptoms after receiving her measles vaccine.

The statement above states a controversial idea as fact without adequate evidence to back it up. Specifically, it makes a false claim of cause and effect about an incident that has no clear causal relationship.

Any claim that is not supported by sufficient evidence is an example of **faulty reasoning**.

Type of Faulty Reasoning	Definition	Example	Explanation
Circular Reasoning	Restating the argument in different words instead of providing evidence	Baseball is the best game in the world because it is more fun than any other game.	Here, everything after the word *because* says approximately the same thing as everything before it. It looks like the author is providing a reason, but no evidence has actually been offered.
Either/Or Fallacy	Presenting an issue as if it involves only two choices when in fact it is not so simple	Women should focus on motherhood, not careers.	This statement assumes that women cannot do both. It also assumes that no woman needs a career in order to provide for her children.
Overgeneralizations	Making a broad claim based on too little evidence	All elderly people have negative stereotypes of teenagers.	This statement lumps a whole category of people into a group and claims the whole group shares the same belief—always an unlikely prospect.

Most texts about evaluating arguments focus on faulty reasoning and false statements of fact. But arguments that attempt to misrepresent facts as opinions are equally suspicious. A careful reader should be skeptical of any text that denies clear physical evidence or questions the truth of events that have been widely verified.

Assumptions and Biases

A well-reasoned argument should be supported by facts, logic, and clearly explained opinions. But most arguments are also based on **assumptions,** or unstated and unproven ideas about what is true. Consider the following argument:

Argument: To improve equality of opportunity for all children, schools in underprivileged areas should receive as much taxpayer funding as schools in wealthy districts.

This argument is based on several assumptions. First is the assumption that all children should have equal opportunities. Another is that taxpayer-funded public schools are the best way to provide these opportunities. Whether or not you disagree with either of these points, it is worth noting that the second idea in particular is not the only way to proceed. Readers who examine the assumptions behind an argument can sometimes find points of disagreement even if an author's claims and logic are otherwise sound.

Examining an author's assumptions can also reveal a writer's biases. A **bias** is a preconceived idea that makes a person more likely to show unfair favor for certain thoughts, people, or groups. Because every person has a different experience of the world, every person has a different set of biases. For example, a person who has traveled widely may feel differently about world political events than someone who has always lived in one place.

Virtually all writing is biased to some degree. However, effective writing attempts to avoid bias as much as possible. Writing that is highly biased may be based on poor assumptions that render the entire argument invalid.

Highly biased writing often includes overgeneralizations. Words like *all, always, never,* and so on may indicate that the writer is overstating a point. While these words can exist in true statements, unbiased writing is more likely to qualify ideas using words like *usually, often,* and *rarely.*

Another quality of biased writing is excessively emotional word choice. When writers insult people who disagree with them or engage the emotions in a way that feels manipulative, they are being biased.

Biased: Power-hungry politicians don't care that their standardized testing requirements are producing a generation of overanxious, incurious, impractical kids.

Less biased: Politicians need to recognize that current standardized testing requirements are causing severe anxiety and other negative effects in children.

Biased writing may also reflect stereotypical thinking. A **stereotype** is a particularly harmful type of bias that applies specifically to groups of people. Stereotypical thinking is behind racism, sexism, homophobia, and so on. Even people who do not consider themselves prejudiced can use language that reflects common stereotypes. For example, the negative use of the word *crazy* reflects a stereotype against people with mental illnesses.

Historically, writers in English have used male nouns and pronouns to indicate all people. Revising such language for more inclusivity is considered more effective in contemporary writing.

Biased: The history of the human race proves that man is a violent creature.

Less biased: The history of the human race proves that people are violent.

Let's Review!

- A text meant to convince someone of something is making an argument.
- Arguments may employ both facts and opinions.
- Effective arguments must use valid reasoning.
- Arguments are based on assumptions that may be reasonable or highly biased.
- Almost all writing is biased to some degree, but strong writing makes an effort to eliminate bias.

EVALUATING AND INTEGRATING DATA

Effective readers do more than absorb and analyze the content of sentences, paragraphs, and chapters. They recognize the importance of features that stand out in and around the text, and they understand and integrate knowledge from visual features like maps and charts.

Text Features

Elements that stand out from a text are called **text features**. Text features perform many vital functions.

- **Introducing the Topic and Organizing Information**

> **COMPARE!**
> The title on a fictional work does not always state the topic explicitly. While some titles do this, others are more concerned with hinting at a theme or setting up the tone.

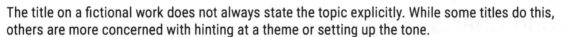

- *Titles* – The title of a nonfiction text typically introduces the topic. Titles are guiding features of organization because they give clues about what is and is not covered. The title of this section, "Text Features," covers exactly that—not, for example, implicit ideas.
- *Headings and Subheadings* – Headings and subheadings provide subtopic information about supporting points and let readers scan to see how information is organized. The subheadings of this page organize text features according to the functions they perform.

- **Helping the Reader Find Information**

- *Table of Contents* – The table of contents of a long work lists chapter titles and other large-scale information so readers can predict the content. This helps readers to determine whether or not a text will be useful to them and to find sections relevant to their research.
- *Index* – In a book, the index is an alphabetical list of topics covered, complete with page numbers where the topics are discussed. Readers looking for information on one small subtopic can check the index to find out which pages to view.
- *Footnotes and Endnotes* – When footnotes and endnotes list sources, they allow the reader to find and evaluate the information an author is citing.

- **Emphasizing Concepts**

- *Formatting Features* – Authors may use formatting features such as *italics*, **boldfacing** or underlining to emphasize a word, phrase, or other important information in a text.
- *Bulleting and numbering* – Bullet points and numbered lists set off information and allow readers to scan for bits of information they do not know. It also helps to break down a list of steps.

- **Presenting Information and Illustrating Ideas**

  - *Graphic Elements* – Charts, graphs, diagrams, and other graphic elements present data succinctly, illustrate complex ideas, or otherwise convey information that would be difficult to glean from text alone.

- **Providing Peripheral Information**

  - *Sidebars* – Sidebars are text boxes that contain information related to the topic but not essential to the overall point.

  - *Footnotes and Endnotes* – Some footnotes and endnotes contain information that is not essential to the development of the main point but may nevertheless interest readers and researchers.[1]

FUN FACT!

Online, a sidebar is sometimes called a *doobly doo*.

P.S. This is an example of a sidebar.

Maps and Charts

To read maps and charts, you need to understand what the labels, symbols, and pictures mean. You also need to know how to make decisions using the information they contain.

Maps

Maps are stylized pictures of places as seen from above. A map may have a box labeled "Key" or "Legend" that provides information about the meanings of colors, lines, or symbols. On the map below, the key shows that a solid line is a road and a dotted line is a trail.

There may also be a line labeled "scale" that helps you figure out how far you need to travel to get from one point on the map to another. In the example below, an inch is only 100 feet, so a trip from one end to the other is not far.

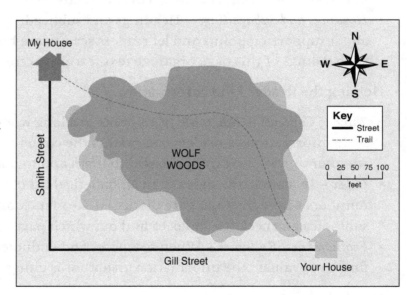

Some maps, including the example above, have compasses that show directions. If no compass is pictured, assume the top of the map is north.

---

[1] Anthony Grafton's book *The Footnote: A Curious History* is an in-depth history of the origins and development of the footnote. (Also, this is an example of a footnote.)

Charts

Nutrition Facts Labels

Nutrition facts labels are charts many people see daily, but not everyone knows how to read them. The top third of the label lists calorie counts, serving sizes, and amount of servings in a package. If a package contains more than one serving, a person who eats the entire contents of the package may be consuming many times the number of calories listed per serving.

The label below lists the content of nutrients such as fats and carbohydrates, and so on. According to the label, a person who eats one serving of the product in the package will ingest 30 mg of cholesterol, or 10% of the total cholesterol he or she should consume in a day.

KEEP IN MIND . . .

The percentages on a Nutrition Facts label do not (and are not meant to) add up to 100. Instead, they show how much of a particular nutrient is contained in a serving of the product, as a proportion of a single person's Daily Value for that nutrient. The Daily Value is the total amount of a nutrient a person is supposed to eat in a day, based on a 2000-calorie diet.

In general, a percentage of 5% or less is considered low, whereas a percentage of 20% or more is considered high. A higher percentage can be good or bad, depending on whether or not a person should be trying to get more of a particular ingredient. People need to get plenty of vitamins, minerals, and fiber. In contrast, most people need to limit their intake of fat, cholesterol, and sodium.

Tables

Tables organize information into vertical columns and horizontal rows. Below is a table that shows how much water falls on areas of various sizes when it rains one inch. It shows, for instance, that a 40' x 70' roof receives 1,743 gallons of rain during a one-inch rainfall event.

Area	Area (square miles)	Area (square kilometers)	Amount of Water (gallons)	Amount of Water (liters)
My roof 40 x 70 feet	.0001	.000257	1,743 gallons	6,601 liters
1 acre (1 square mile = 640 acres)	.00156	.004	27,154 gallons	102,789 liters
1 square mile	1	2.6	17.38 million gallons	65.78 million liters
Atlanta, Georgia	132.4	342.9	2.293 billion gallons	8.68 billion liters
United States	3,537,438	9,161,922	61,474 billion gallons	232,700 billion liters

Let's Review!

- Readers must understand how and why text features make certain information stand out from the text.
- Readers must understand and interpret the content of maps and charts.

Types of Passages, Text Structures, Genre and Theme

To read effectively, you must understand what kind of text you are reading and how it is structured. You must also be able to look behind the text to find its deeper meanings.

Types of Passages

There are many ways of breaking texts down into categories. To do this, you need to consider the author's **purpose**, or what the text exists to do. Most texts exist to inform, persuade, or entertain. You also need to consider what the text does—whether it tells a story, describes facts, or develops a point of view.

Type of Passage	Examples
Narrative writing tells a story. The story can be fictional, or it can describe real events. The primary purpose of narrative writing is to entertain.	• An autobiography • A memoir • A short story • A novel
Expository writing provides an explanation or a description. Many academic essays and informational nonfiction books are expository writing. Stylistically, expository writing is highly varied. Although the explanations can be dry and methodical, many writers use an artful or entertaining style. Expository writing is nonfiction. Its primary purpose is to inform.	• A book about a historical event • An essay describing the social impacts of a new technology • A description of changing gender roles in marriages • A philosophical document exploring the nature of truth.
Technical writing explains a complex process or mechanism. Whereas expository writing is often academic, technical writing is used in practical settings such as businesses. The style of a technical document is almost always straightforward and impersonal. Technical writing is nonfiction, and its purpose is to inform.	• Recipes • Instructions • User manuals • Process descriptions
Persuasive writing makes an argument. It asks readers to believe something or do something. Texts that make judgments, such as movie reviews, are persuasive because they are attempting to convince readers to accept a point of view. Texts that suggest a plan are also persuasive because they are trying to convince readers to take an action. As the name "persuasive writing" indicates, the author's primary purpose is to persuade.	• Op-ed newspaper articles • Book reviews • Project proposals • Advertisements • Persuasive essays

---

BE CAREFUL!

Many texts have more than one purpose.

A text that tells a story is usually meant to entertain, but it can also be meant to persuade. For example, there is a well-known story called "Never Cry Wolf" about a boy who habitually lies. At the end, when he needs help, nobody believes him. This story is meant to entertain, but it is also trying to convince readers not to tell lies.

Similarly, many explanatory texts are meant to inform readers in an entertaining way. For example, a nonfiction author may describe a scientific topic using humor and wacky examples to make it fun for popular audiences to read.

Also, expository writing can look similar to persuasive writing, especially when it touches on topics that are controversial or emotional. For example, if an essay says social media is changing society, many readers assume it means social media is changing society *in a negative way*. If the writing makes this kind of value judgment or uses words like *should,* it is persuasive writing. But if the author is merely describing changes, the text is expository.

Text Structures

Authors rarely present ideas within a text in a random order. Instead, they organize their thoughts carefully. To read effectively, you must be able to recognize the **structure** of a text. That is, you need to identify the strategies authors use to organize their ideas. The five most common text structures are listed below.

Text Structure	Examples
In a **sequence** text, an author explains what happened first, second, third, and so on. In other words, a sequence text is arranged in **chronological order**, or time order. This type of text may describe events that have already happened or events that may happen in the future.	• A story about a birthday party. • A historical paper about World War II. • A list of instructions for baking a cake. • A series of proposed steps in a plan for business expansion.
A **compare/contrast** text explains the similarities and differences between two or more subjects. Authors may compare and contrast people, places, ideas, events, cultures, and so on.	• An essay describing the similarities and differences between women's experiences in medieval Europe and Asia. • A section in an op-ed newspaper article explaining the similarities and differences between two types of gun control.
A **cause/effect** text describes an event or action and its results. The causes and effects discussed can be actual or theoretical. That is, the author can describe the results of a historical event or predict the results of a possible future event.	• An explanation of ocean acidification and the coral bleaching that results. • A paper describing a proposed new law and its likely effects on the economy.
A **problem-solution** text presents a problem and outlines a solution. Sometimes it also predicts or analyzes the results of the solution. The solution can be something that already happened or a plan the author is proposing. Note that a problem can sometimes be expressed in terms of a wish or desire that the solution fulfills.	• An explanation of the problems smallpox caused and the strategies scientists used to eradicate it. • A business plan outlining a group of potential customers and the strategy a company should use to get their business.

Text Structure	Examples
A **description** text creates a mental picture for the reader by presenting concrete details in a coherent order. Description texts are usually arranged spatially. For instance, authors may describe the subject from top to bottom, or they may describe the inside first and then the outside, etc.	• An explanation of the appearance of a character in a story. • A paragraph in a field guide detailing the features of a bird. • A section on an instruction sheet describing how the final product should look.

CONNECTIONS

Different types of texts can use the same structures.

1. A story about a birthday party is a narrative, and its purpose is to entertain.
2. A historical paper about a war is an expository text meant to inform.
3. A list of instructions for baking a cake is a technical text meant to inform.
4. A series of proposed steps in a plan for business expansion is a persuasive text meant to persuade.

If all of these texts list ideas in chronological order, explaining what happened (or what may happen in the future) first, second, third, and so on, they are all using a sequence structure.

Genre and Theme

Literature can be organized into categories called **genres**. The two major genres of literature are fiction and nonfiction.

Fiction is made up. It can be broken down into many sub-genres, or sub-categories. The following are some of the common ones:

- Short story – Short work of fiction.
- Novel – Book-length work of fiction.
- Science fiction – A story set in the future
- Romance – A love story
- Mystery – A story that answers a concrete question, often about who committed a crime
- Mythology – A traditional story that reflects cultural traditions and beliefs but does not usually teach an explicit lesson
- Legends – Traditional stories that are presented as histories, even though they often contain fantastical or magical elements
- Fables – Traditional stories meant to teach an explicit lesson

> **COMPARE!**
>
> The differences between myths and fables are sometimes hard to discern.
>
> Myths are often somewhat religious in nature. For instance, stories about Ancient Greek gods and goddesses are myths. These stories reflect cultural beliefs, for example by showing characters being punished for failing to please their gods. But the lesson is implicit. These stories do not usually end with a moral lesson that says to readers, "Do not displease the gods!"
>
> Fables are often for children, and they usually end with a sentence stating an explicit moral. For example, there's a story called "The Tortoise and the Hare," in which a tortoise and a hare agree to have a race. The hare, being a fast animal, gets cocky and takes a lot of breaks while the tortoise plods slowly toward the finish line without stopping. Because the tortoise keeps going, it eventually wins. The story usually ends with the moral, "Slow and steady win the race."

Nonfiction is true. Like fiction, it can be broken down into many sub-genres. The following are some of the common ones:

- Autobiography and memoir – The author's own life story
- Biography – Someone else's life story (not the author's)
- Histories – True stories about real events from the past
- Criticism and reviews – A response or judgment on another piece of writing or art
- Essay – A short piece describing the author's outlook or point of view.

> **CONNECTIONS**
>
> Everything under "Fiction" and several items under "Nonfiction" above are examples of narrative writing. We use labels like "narrative" and "persuasive" largely when we discuss writing tasks or the author's purpose. We could use these labels here too, but at the moment we're more concerned with the words that are most commonly used in discussions about literature's deeper meanings.

Literature reflects the human experience. Texts from different genres often share similar **themes**, or deeper meanings. Texts from different cultures do too. For example, a biography of a famous civil rights activist may highlight the same qualities of heroism and interconnectedness that appear in a work of mythology from Ancient India. Other common themes in literature may relate to war, love, survival, justice, suffering, growing up, and other experiences that are accessible to virtually all human beings.

Many students confuse the term *theme* with the term *moral*. A **moral** is an explicit message contained in the text, like "Don't lie" or "Crime doesn't pay." Morals are a common feature of fables and other traditional stories meant to teach lessons to children. Themes, in contrast, are implicit. Readers must consider the clues in the story and figure out themes for themselves. Because of this, themes are debatable. For testing purposes, questions focus on themes that are clearly and consistently indicated by clues within the text.

Let's Review!

- Written texts can be organized into the following categories: narrative, expository, technical, and persuasive.
- Texts of all categories may use the following organizational schemes or structures: sequence, compare/contrast, cause/effect, problem-solution, description.
- Literature can be organized into genres including fiction, nonfiction, and many sub-genres.
- Literature across genres and cultures often reflects the same deeper meanings, or themes.

> **KEEP IN MIND . . .**
>
> The text structures above do not always work in isolation. Authors often combine two or more structures within one text. For example, a business plan could be arranged in a problem-solution structure as the author describes what the business wants to achieve and how she proposes to achieve it. The "how" portion could also use a sequence structure as the author lists the steps to follow first, second, third, and so on.

TABE PRACTICE EXAM 1

SECTION I. LANGUAGE

1. Which word in the following sentence is an adjective?

   The opera singer's voice, poise, and costume were all perfect.

   A. voice

   B. poise

   C. costume

   D. perfect

2. Select the parts of speech of the underlined words in the following sentence.

   I had an <u>early</u> meeting, so I woke up <u>early</u>.

   A. Adverb, adverb

   B. Adverb, adjective

   C. Adjective, adverb

   D. Adjective, adjective

3. Which of the following is correct?

   A. May

   B. Spring

   C. easter

   D. sunday

4. Fill in the blank with the correctly capitalized form.

   My favorite book in the Harry Potter series is _____.

   A. *harry potter and the prisoner of azkaban*

   B. *Harry Potter and the prisoner of azkaban*

   C. *Harry Potter And The Prisoner Of Azkaban*

   D. *Harry Potter and the Prisoner of Azkaban*

5. What does the underlined coordinating conjunction in the sentence below connect?

   We had a dry summer, <u>so</u> the crops didn't do well.

   A. Dependent clauses

   B. Independent clauses

   C. Prepositional phrases

   D. Gerunds

6. Identify the prepositional phrase in the following sentence.

   The show got great reviews, so we plan to see it on Saturday.

   A. got great reviews

   B. so we plan

   C. see it

   D. on Saturday

7. Select the context clue from the following sentence that helps you define the word <u>insatiable</u>.

   The teenager has such an insatiable appetite that he eats frequently.

   A. teenager

   B. appetite

   C. eats

   D. frequently

8. Select the word from the following sentence that has more than one meaning.

   After he failed his physics test, my brother began to channel his anger toward me.

   A. failed

   B. test

   C. channel

   D. anger

9. **Select the correct definition of the underlined word that has more than one meaning in the sentence.**

    The nursing students were learning about the human <u>figure</u> with a life-sized dummy and other plastic models.

    A. A shape or form

    B. A person who is regarded in a special way

    C. A diagram or picture

    D. A value expressed in numbers

10. **Select the direct object of the underlined verb.**

    Andrei was happy to help his daughter and her fiance <u>plan</u> their wedding.

    A. was happy

    B. to help

    C. his daughter and her fiance

    D. their wedding

11. **Select the verb that acts on the underlined direct object.**

    We decided that we should walk <u>the dog</u> before going to the restaurant.

    A. decided

    B. should

    C. walk

    D. going

12. **Which of the following verbs <u>cannot</u> take a direct object?**

    A. Snore

    B. Watch

    C. Choose

    D. Bake

13. **Which word does the underlined modifier describe?**

    I looked up to Marvin, <u>who was a year older</u>.

    A. I

    B. looked

    C. up

    D. Marvin

14. **Identify the dangling modifier in the following sentence.**

    After reading the book, the movie that just came out must be pretty bad.

    A. After reading the book

    B. the movie

    C. that just came out

    D. must be really bad

15. **How many modifiers describe the underlined word in the following sentence?**

    Pass that large silver <u>bowl</u>.

    A. 1

    B. 2

    C. 3

    D. 4

16. **Which of the following nouns can be made plural by simply adding -s?**

    A. Fox

    B. Frog

    C. Cherry

    D. Potato

17. **What part of speech is the underlined word in the following sentence?**

    Douglas served on the <u>Supreme Court</u> for 36 years.

    A. Noun

    B. Pronoun

    C. Adjective

    D. Preposition

18. **Which word in the following sentence is a pronoun?**

    The driver checked her side mirror.

    A. The

    B. her

    C. side

    D. driver

19. **Select the pronoun that could be used in the following sentence.**

    Mrs. Sato, ____ lives down the street, is 99 years old.

    A. she

    B. who

    C. which

    D. whom

20. **Which sentence is incorrect?**

    A. I hate you!

    B. When does the movie start?

    C. I go to bed early so I do not feel tired.

    D. You should drink eight glasses of water a day.

21. **What is missing from the following sentence?**

    He asked, When is the assignment due?

    A. There should be quotation marks.

    B. There needs to be a semicolon after asked.

    C. There should be a comma after assignment.

    D. Nothing is missing.

22. **An amicable person is one who is**

    A. timid.

    B. friendly.

    C. capable.

    D. uncertain.

23. **Select the meaning of the underlined word in the sentence.**

    The city's government is infamous for being corrupt and dishonest.

    A. Content

    B. Regretful

    C. Notorious

    D. Apologetic

24. **Which of the following root words means foot?**

    A. ped

    B. man

    C. corp

    D. post

25. **Which of the following spellings is correct?**

    A. Argument

    B. Arguemint

    C. Arguement

    D. Arguemant

26. **What is the correct plural of half?**

    A. Half

    B. Halfs

    C. Halfes

    D. Halves

27. **Which part of the following sentence is the predicate?**

    Mai and her friend Oksana love to ride roller coasters.

    A. Mai and her friend Oksana

    B. and her friend Oksana

    C. love to ride roller coasters

    D. roller coasters

28. **Select the subject that would be incorrect in the following sentence.**

    ____ are excited about the upcoming election.

    A. He

    B. We

    C. You

    D. They

29. **Select the correct verbs to complete the following sentence.**

    My dentist, who I ____ visited for years, ____ suddenly disappeared.

    A. has, has

    B. have, has

    C. has, have

    D. have, have

30. **The following words have the same denotation. Which word has a positive connotation?**

    A. Assertive

    B. Dictatorial

    C. Domineering

    D. Overbearing

31. **Quaff : Beverage :: Garnish : _____**

    A. Plate

    B. Closet

    C. Canvas

    D. Garden

32. Adding which prefix to <u>intentional</u> would make the antonym of the word?

    A. De-   C. Dis-

    B. Un-   D. Mis-

33. Identify the dependent clause in the following sentence.

    Joe always did his homework before he went to bed.

    A. Went to bed

    B. Before he went to bed

    C. Joe always did his homework

    D. Did his homework

34. How would you connect the following clauses?

    She gave her dog a long walk.

    He slept well that night.

    A. She gave her a dog a long walk, and he slept well that night.

    B. She gave her dog a long walk, but he slept well that night.

    C. She gave her dog a long walk, or he slept well that night.

    D. She gave her dog a long walk, yet he slept well that night.

35. Fill in the blank with the correct subordinating conjunction.

    I had a bad stomach flu but started to regain my appetite, _____ is good news.

    A. so   C. which

    B. that   D. whereas

36. Which of the following is an example of a compound sentence?

    A. The Jankowskis typically go out for Italian food, tonight they tried Thai.

    B. The Jankowskis typically go out for Italian food and tonight they tried Thai.

    C. The Jankowskis typically go out for Italian food, but tonight they tried Thai.

    D. The Jankowskis typically go out for Italian food even though tonight they tried Thai.

37. Which of the following uses a conjunction to combine the sentences below so the focus is on Tony preparing for his job interview?

    Tony prepared well for his job interview. Tony ended up getting an offer.

    A. Tony ended up getting an offer; he prepared for his job interview.

    B. Tony prepared well for his job interview, he ended up getting an offer.

    C. Tony prepared well for his job interview and he ended up getting an offer.

    D. Tony ended up getting an offer because he prepared for his job interview.

38. Which of the following options correctly fixes the run-on sentence below?

Texting while driving is reckless it could cost you your life.

A. Texting while driving is reckless, it could cost you your life.

B. Texting while driving is reckless it. Could cost you your life.

C. Texting while driving. Is reckless, it could cost you your life.

D. Texting while driving is reckless, and it could cost you your life.

39. Select the response that correctly describes both of the underlined verbs.

When a buyer <u>offered</u> 5% below our asking price, our realtor <u>advised</u> us to accept the offer.

A. Helping verbs

B. Past tense verbs

C. Present tense verbs

D. Progressive tense verbs

40. Select the verb that best completes the following sentence.

Katharina didn't ____ her job as an accountant, so she decided to change careers.

A. like

B. likes

C. liken

D. liked

SECTION II. MATHEMATICS

1. Evaluate the expression 397 + 451.

   A. 748　　　　　C. 857

   B. 848　　　　　D. 925

2. Which statement best describes a remainder in division?

   A. The quotient minus the divisor

   B. The product of the dividend and divisor

   C. The difference between the dividend and the quotient

   D. The portion of a dividend not evenly divisible by the divisor

3. Evaluate the expression $12 \div 4 \times 3 + 1$.

   A. 0　　　　　C. 10

   B. 2　　　　　D. 12

4. Find the area in square inches of a pizza with a diameter of 10.5 inches. Round to the nearest hundredth. Use 3.14 for π.

   A. 65.94　　　　　C. 173.09

   B. 86.54　　　　　D. 346.19

5. Find the circumference of a circle in inches with a diameter of 6 inches. Use 3.14 for π.

   A. 9.42　　　　　C. 25.12

   B. 18.84　　　　　D. 37.68

6. What is the intersection of two walls in a room?

   A. A ray　　　　　C. A point

   B. A line　　　　　D. A plane

7. What is the order of rotational symmetry for a parallelogram?

   A. 1　　　　　C. 3

   B. 2　　　　　D. 4

8. Write 62.42% as a fraction.

   A. $\frac{31}{50000}$　　　　　C. $\frac{3121}{50000}$

   B. $\frac{31}{5000}$　　　　　D. $\frac{3121}{5000}$

9. Write $1\frac{11}{20}$ as a percent.

   A. 150%　　　　　C. 200%

   B. 155%　　　　　D. 205%

10. Solve the equation for the unknown, $2(x-4) = 5(x + 2)$.

    A. −24　　　　　C. −6

    B. −12　　　　　D. −2

11. Solve the inequality for the unknown, $\frac{1}{4}x - \frac{1}{3}(x + 2) \leq \frac{1}{12}(2x + 3) + x - 1$.

    A. $x \leq -\frac{1}{15}$　　　　　C. $x \leq \frac{1}{15}$

    B. $x \geq -\frac{1}{15}$　　　　　D. $x \geq \frac{1}{15}$

12. **Solve the system of equations by graphing,** $y = -2x + 3$
    $y = 3$.

A.

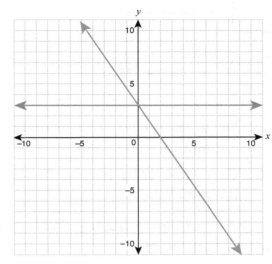

B.

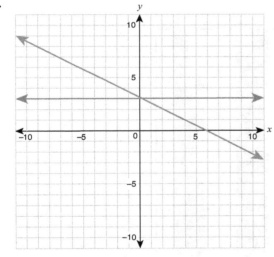

C.

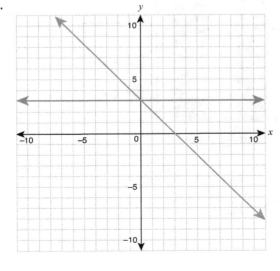

D.

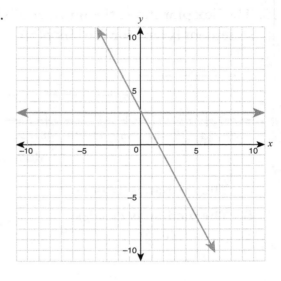

13. **Solve the system of equations,**
    $x - 5y = -21$
    $3x + y = 33$.

    A. (4, 1)   C. (9, 6)

    B. (1, 4)   D. (6, 9)

14. **If the multiple of some positive number is prime, which statement about that positive number is true?**

    A. The positive number is prime.

    B. The positive number is equal to 0.

    C. The positive number is composite.

    D. None of the above.

15. **Identify the variable from a census study that is categorical.**

    A. Age   C. Family size

    B. Zip code   D. Annual income

16. The box plot shows the number of weekly sales by a business during the year. Which statement is true for the box plot?

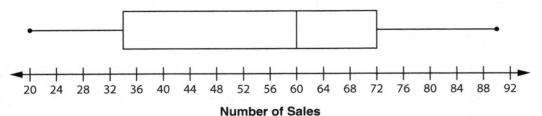

A. The median is 34 sales.

B. The median is 72 sales.

C. The difference between the maximum and minimum is 40 sales.

D. The difference between the maximum and minimum is 70 sales.

17. The bar chart shows the number of boys and girls who participate in sports. What is the greatest difference between numbers of participants in any year?

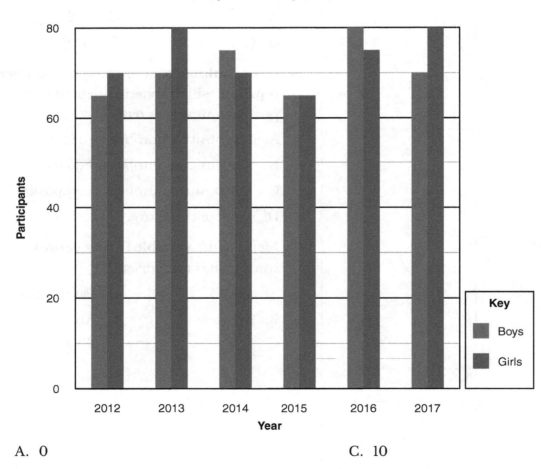

A. 0

B. 5

C. 10

D. 15

18. Elementary school teachers were told that children's parents were high school graduates, did not complete college, or were college graduates. Then, the children's grades were compared. Determine the dependent variable.

A. College graduate

B. Children's grades

C. High school graduate

D. Did not complete college

19. A sand timer is made up of two cones. What is the volume if the diameter and height of one cone is 30 millimeters?

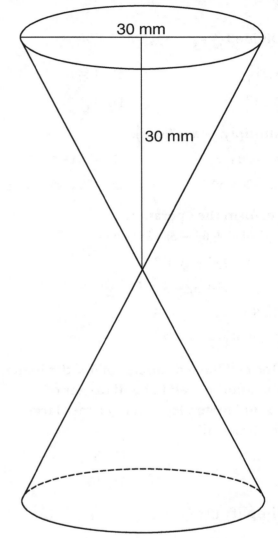

30 mm

30 mm

A. 2,250π cubic millimeters

B. 4,500π cubic millimeters

C. 9,000π cubic millimeters

D. 18,000π cubic millimeters

20. Find the volume in cubic inches of a cylinder with a circumference of 14π inches and a height of 12 inches.

A. 294π

B. 588π

C. 1,176π

D. 2,352π

21. Multiply $\frac{2}{5} \times 3$.

   A. $\frac{2}{15}$ C. $2\frac{3}{5}$

   B. $1\frac{1}{5}$ D. $3\frac{2}{5}$

22. Divide $1\frac{9}{14} \div \frac{3}{5}$.

   A. $\frac{69}{70}$ C. $1\frac{27}{70}$

   B. $1\frac{1}{3}$ D. $2\frac{31}{42}$

23. Multiply, $-4x^2y^2(5xy^3)$.

   A. $-20x^2y^5$ C. $-20x^2y^6$

   B. $-20x^3y^5$ D. $-20x^3y^6$

24. Perform the operation,
    $(3y^3-4y^2 + 6y + 3)-(2y^3-3y)$.

   A. $5y^3-4y^2 + 3y + 3$

   B. $y^3-4y^2 + 3y + 3$

   C. $5y^3-4y^2 + 9y + 3$

   D. $y^3-4y^2 + 9y + 3$

25. One cell has a diameter of 5×10^{-8} meter, and another cell has a diameter of 6×10^{-9} meter. How many times larger is the first cell?

   A. 2   C. 8

   B. 4   D. 16

26. Simplify $(9x^{-2}y^3)^2$.

   A. $\frac{1}{81x^4y^6}$ C. $\frac{81x^4}{y^6}$

   B. $\frac{81y^6}{x^4}$ D. $81x^4y^6$

27. Which ratio is equal to 31%?

   A. 3:10   C. 3:1

   B. 31:100   D. 31:1

28. If a baseball is 15 feet high when a stopwatch reads 3.2 seconds and 30 feet high when the stopwatch reads 3.6 seconds, what is its vertical speed (that is, rate of change of height)? Assume the speed is constant between 3.2 and 3.6 seconds on the stopwatch.

   A. 0.03 feet per second

   B. 15 feet per second

   C. 37.5 feet per second

   D. 75 feet per second

29. A yield sign in the shape of a triangle has a base length of 90 centimeters and a height of 80 centimeters. What is the area in square centimeters?

   A. 1,800   C. 5,400

   B. 3,600   D. 7,200

30. A park is in the shape of a square with side lengths of 175 yards. One corner of the park is on the coordinate plane as $(-50,-50)$. What could be two coordinates of the square?

   A. $(-50, -125), (-50,125)$

   B. $(-50, 125), (125,-50)$

   C. $(50, 50), (-50, 50)$

   D. $(50, 50), (50, -50)$

31. Solve the equation by completing the square, $x^2 + 10x-10 = 0$.

   A. $-5 \pm \sqrt{10}$ C. $-5 \pm \sqrt{35}$

   B. $5 \pm \sqrt{10}$ D. $5 \pm \sqrt{35}$

32. Solve the equation by the quadratic formula, $x^2 + 10x + 8 = 0$.

   A. −0.88 and 9.13

   B. 0.88 and −9.13

   C. −0.88 and −9.13

   D. 0.88 and 9.13

33. A small landscaping company mows lawns and has three 5.4-gallon gas cans. One day, the landscapers empty the gas cans three times. How many gallons of gas did they use?

   A. 10.8   C. 32.4

   B. 16.2   D. 48.6

34. A pair of jeans with tax costs $39.97, and a shirt with tax costs $18.49. What is the amount of change for a pair of jeans and two shirts if playing with a $100 bill?

   A. $23.05   C. $41.54

   B. $36.98   D. $60.03

35. Convert 4 tons to pounds.

   A. 2,000 pounds   C. 8,000 pounds

   B. 4,000 pounds   D. 10,000 pounds

36. Convert 147 liters to kiloliters.

   A. 0.147 kiloliters   C. 1,470 kiloliters

   B. 1.47 kiloliters   D. 147,000 kiloliters

37. Identify the sampling technique that is a convenience sample.

   A. A group of students selected by a principal

   B. A group of students selected by their grade point average

   C. A group of students selected by their after-school availability

   D. A group of students selected by a random number generator

38. Identify the study that is a survey.

   A. A researcher interviews all nurses at all hospitals.

   B. A researcher interviews all nurses at all hospitals in the state.

   C. A researcher interviews all nurses at 10 hospitals that are near her.

   D. A researcher interviews all nurses at 10 hospitals in different regions.

39. A spinner is labeled 1–10. What is the probability of landing on a multiple of 3?

   A. $\frac{1}{10}$ C. $\frac{3}{10}$

   B. $\frac{1}{5}$ D. $\frac{2}{5}$

40. The table below shows the value of the prizes and the probability of winning a prize in a state contest.

Prize	$100	$1,000	$10,000	$100,000
Probability	1 in 500	1 in 25,000	1 in 100,000	1 in 2,500,000

Calculate the expected value.

A. $0.20

B. $0.38

C. $0.40

D. $0.76

SECTION III. READING

Read the following passage and answer questions 1-3.

Every time I visit the bookstore, I find a new science fiction title about post-apocalyptic survivors taking refuge in New York City's subway tunnels. Some of these survival stories are fun to read, but they have a pesky plausibility problem: if society collapses, those subway tunnels won't be there anymore—at least not for long. On a typical day in a functioning New York City, a crew of engineers works around the clock to pump about 13 million gallons of water out of the subway system, and a major rain event pushes that number up fast. What happens if you take the engineers—and the electricity to work the sump pumps—out of the equation? The first big storm will flood those tunnels, probably for good. At that point, any survivors left underground will have to grow gills or head for the surface.

1. **Which of the following is the best title for this passage?**

   A. A Visit to a Bookstore

   B. The Science of Growing Gills

   C. A Refuge in Fiction, But Not in Fact

   D. The Best Science Fiction of the Year

2. **Which graphic element would most clearly illustrate the author's point?**

   A. A schematic showing the depth and volume of all of New York City's subway tunnels

   B. A graph comparing the ridership of New York City's subways with those of other major American cities

   C. A table showing how much water runs through the New York City subway system in varying conditions

   D. A New York City subway map showing emergency exits and detailing procedures for exiting the system during a flood

3. **Which information would belong in a sidebar alongside this text?**

   A. An illustration showing how a family of people might look if they all had gills behind their ears

   B. A description of a subway's electrified third rail and an explanation of how it works to power the train

   C. A list of science fiction novels about people living in subway tunnels in a post-apocalyptic world

   D. A description of the job qualifications of a subway engineer who works the pumps to keep the tunnels functional

4. Carla is trying to limit her calorie intake. When she buys a bottle of soda, she is pleased to see a low value of 100 calories per serving. Before she pours herself a glass, she should check the number of:

    A. servings per bottle.

    B. calories per gram of fat.

    C. calories per gram of sugar.

    D. servings in a glass of water.

Read the following paragraph and answer questions 5-8.

The idea of raising children in prison is controversial, but well-run prison nursery programs can actually be beneficial. A study of preschool age children showed that anxiety and depression are common among young children who are separated from their mothers at birth and reunited later. In contrast, babies who spent brief sentences of two years or less behind bars with their mothers showed greater resilience and stronger attachments.

According to a nationwide analysis of women who participated in prison nursery programs, the benefits for mothers are even clearer than the benefits to children. Women who were allowed to remain with their infants during prison sentences were less likely to be convicted of another crime and less likely to use drugs in the five years after release. They were more likely to continue their education in prison and more likely to find employment on the outside. Mothers involved in prison nursery programs also reported better mental health and greater confidence in their own parenting skills.

5. **What is one assumption behind the passage?**

    A. Imprisoned mothers should take parenting classes to learn how to raise children.

    B. Some people disagree with the idea of allowing mothers to raise children in prison.

    C. The needs of incarcerated mothers are more important than the needs of their babies.

    D. Society should protect the health and well-being of children born to incarcerated mothers.

6. **What is the primary argument of the passage?**

    A. Young children should not be forced to live in prisons.

    B. Society must promote the health and safety of children.

    C. Letting imprisoned mothers keep their babies can be helpful.

    D. It is bad for children but good for mothers if children live in prison.

7. Consider the following sentence from the passage:

Mothers involved in prison nursery programs also reported better mental health and greater confidence in their own parenting skills.

Is this statement a fact or an opinion? Why?

A. An opinion because it shares information about confidence, which is an emotion.

B. A fact because it states verifiable information about how women reported they felt.

C. A fact because it focuses on information from medical records rather than faulty memories.

D. An opinion because it relies on human input rather than objective sources like computer records.

8. **Which statement expresses an opinion?**

A. A study of preschool age children showed that anxiety and depression are common among young children who are separated from their mothers at birth and reunited later.

B. The idea of raising children in prison is controversial, but well-run prison nursery programs can actually be beneficial.

C. Mothers involved in prison nursery programs also reported better mental health and greater confidence in their own parenting skills.

D. Women who were allowed to remain with their infants during prison sentences were less likely to be convicted of another crime and less likely to use drugs after release.

9. **Which of the following sentences uses the MOST informal language?**

A. I must go to school.

B. I have to go to school.

C. I need to go to school.

D. I gotta go to school.

10. **In which of the following situations would it be best to use informal language?**

A. A charity event

B. A football game

C. A job interview

D. A dentist's office

11. **In which of the following situations would it be best to use informal language?**

A. At brunch

B. Talking to a professor

C. Giving a presentation

D. Giving a professional talk

12. **Which of the following sentences uses the MOST formal language?**

A. I want to tell you my business plan.

B. I am writing to explain my business plan.

C. I'm telling you my business plan.

D. I'm explaining my business plan.

Please read the text below and answer questions 13-17.

It is perhaps unsurprising that fad diets are so common given the level of obesity in American society. But over the long term, most fad diets are harmful both to the health and to the waistline. Many such diets advocate cutting out one major nutrient, such as fats or carbohydrates. Others suggest fasting over long periods or eating from fixed menu options that may not meet the body's needs. Most of these diets are highly impractical, and many lead directly or indirectly to binge eating and other unhealthy behaviors.

13. **The topic of this paragraph is:**

    A. fasting.

    B. obesity.

    C. fad diets.

    D. binge eating.

14. **The topic sentence of this paragraph is:**

    A. But over the long term, most fad diets are harmful both to the health and to the waistline.

    B. Many such diets advocate cutting out one major nutrient, such as fats or carbohydrates.

    C. It is perhaps unsurprising that fad diets are so common given the level of obesity in American society.

    D. Most of these diets are highly impractical, and many lead directly or indirectly to binge eating and other unhealthy behaviors.

15. **If the author added a description of a man who attempted several fad diets and ended up heavier than ever, what type of information would this be?**

    A. A main idea

    B. A topic sentence

    C. A supporting detail

    D. An off-topic sentence

16. **Read the following description of the paragraph:**

    The author argues unfairly against fad diets without taking their good qualities into account.

    Why is this *not* a valid description of the main idea?

    A. It is not accurate; the author of the paragraph is stating facts, not opinions.

    B. It is not objective; the person summarizing the main idea is adding a judgment.

    C. It is not accurate; the author of the paragraph does not argue against fad diets.

    D. It is not objective; the person summarizing the main idea ignores a sentence about the benefits of dieting.

17. **Why doesn't a statistic about early childhood obesity rates belong in this paragraph?**

    A. It does not directly support the main idea that fad diets are harmful.

    B. Readers might feel hopeless to solve the problem the author identifies.

    C. Statistics should never be used as supporting details in persuasive writing.

    D. It would act as a second topic sentence and confuse readers about the main idea.

Study the flowchart below and answer questions 18-19.

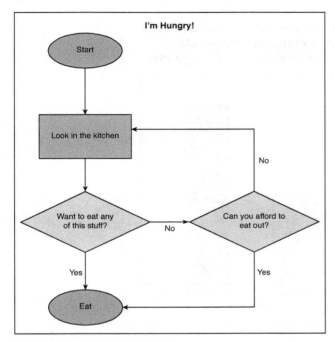

18. **What is the first thing the chart asks you to do if you are hungry?**

    A. Eat.

    B. Look in the kitchen.

    C. Consider whether you can afford to eat out.

    D. Consider whether you want to eat what you have.

19. **According to the flowchart, what do you need to do if you cannot afford to eat out?**

    A. Grow a garden.

    C. Buy a recipe book.

    B. Get a better job.

    D. Find food in the kitchen.

A high school student is presenting research on how gender affects participation in her political science class. Study the graphic elements below and answer questions 20-22.

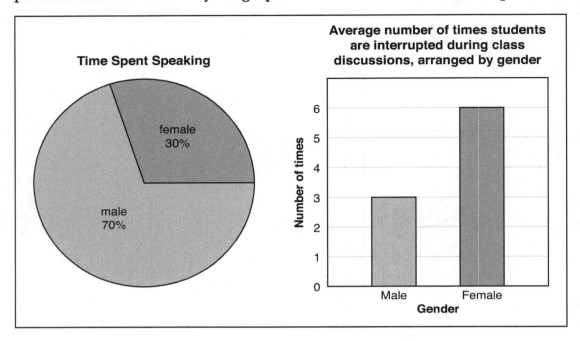

20. Male students spend _____ of class time speaking.

    A. 3%   C. 30%

    B. 6%   D. 70%

21. Which statement accurately describes the average number of interruptions during each class discussion?

    A. Male students are interrupted an average of six times.

    B. Female students are interrupted an average of six times.

    C. Male students interrupt others an average of three times.

    D. Female students interrupt others an average of three times.

22. Which argument does the information in the graphs best support?

    A. Female students do not have as many ideas about political science as male students.

    B. The class should make a greater effort to give students of both genders a fair chance to speak.

    C. Contrary to popular belief, male students face greater gender discrimination in school settings.

    D. There is no substantial difference between male and female students' class participation in discussions.

Read the passage and answer questions 23-26.

Dear Dr. Rodriguez,

I am writing to request that you change my daughter Amelia's chemistry grade. Amelia is a brilliant and capable girl who does not deserve an F in your class. Incidentally, I am sure you recall our family's substantial donation to your school district last year. I was led to believe we would no longer be troubled by petty grade issues or incompetent teachers after I wrote that check. In fact, I feel compelled to forward this message to your superiors to make certain the issue is dealt with promptly, and to ensure that we have no future misunderstandings.

Sincerely,

Violetta D. Johannsen

23. **Which adjective best describes the tone of this passage?**

    A. Friendly   C. Hopeless

    B. Arrogant   D. Respectful

24. **Which phrase from the passage has an openly hostile and superior tone?**

    A. I am writing to request   C. incompetent teachers

    B. brilliant and capable   D. to make certain

25. **What mood would this passage most likely evoke in the chemistry teacher, Dr. Rodriguez?**

    A. Fury   C. Calm

    B. Glee   D. Respect

26. **Which transition word or phrase from the passage adds emphasis to the writer's point?**

    A. And   C. In fact

    B. After   D. Incidentally

27. **Read the sentences below.**

    Jeremiah's lacrosse season had a rocky start. He is determined to score more goals than his teammates this year.

    Which word or phrase, if inserted at the beginning of sentence two, would effectively transition between these two ideas?

    A. Likewise   C. For example

    B. Previously   D. Nevertheless

Read the following text and answer questions 28-31.

Fly Lake is the heart and soul of our town, and it needs our help. The environmental problems are obvious everywhere. The parking lot and path to the lake are strewn with beer cans and other litter. A half-dead grove of oaks bears the scars of a careless visitor's untended fire. Other trees are tagged with spray-painted graffiti. Any visitor who bothers to walk past this depressing scene all the way to the edge of the lake will notice piles of discarded fishing gear—but the fishing is terrible these days. Beneath the surface, hardly anything is still swimming. The lake has long been a source of recreation, tourist revenue, and food for the people of our town, but if current trends continue, it will no longer be able to fulfill any of these roles. For the greater good, we need funding and workers to clean up Fly Lake.

28. This passage is best described as:

A. narrative.

B. technical.

C. persuasive.

D. expository.

29. Which two organizational schemes best describe the structure of the text?

A. Cause/effect and sequence

B. Problem-solution and description

C. Cause/effect and compare/contrast

D. Problem-solution and compare/contrast

30. If this text were to continue for a few more paragraphs, which genre label would best apply to it?

A. Essay

B. Fable

C. History

D. Memoir

31. Which statement best expresses the unstated theme of the passage?

A. People who litter should pay hefty fines.

B. Caring for the environment benefits everyone.

C. If you start a campfire, don't be careless with it.

D. Worthless human beings scar and defile the earth.

Read the following passage and answer questions 32-35.

Adelia stood on the porch in her bathrobe.

"Mr. Snuggles?" she called. "Mr. Snuggles! Come on in, you little vermin."

She peered up and down the street. Sighing, she went back inside and, a moment later, emerged with a metal bowl and a spoon. She rapped on the bowl several times.

"Mr. Snuggles? Breakfast!"

When Mr. Snuggles did not appear, Adelia reached inside and grabbed some keys off a low table. Cinching her bathrobe tightly around her waist, she climbed into the car.

"It's not like I have anything better to do than look for you again," she said.

32. **From the text above, you can infer that Adelia is:**

   A. looking for a pet.

   B. calling her son home.

   C. a kindhearted person.

   D. unconcerned for Mr. Snuggles.

33. **Which detail does not provide evidence to back up the conclusion that Adelia is feeling frustrated?**

   A. She calls Mr. Snuggles "you little vermin."

   B. She has not yet gotten dressed for the day.

   C. She complains about having to search for Mr. Snuggles.

   D. She sighs when Mr. Snuggles does not immediately appear.

34. **Which detail from the text supports the inference that Adelia cares what happens to Mr. Snuggles, even if she is angry at him?**

   A. She goes out to look for him.

   B. She keeps her car keys near the door.

   C. She is joking when she calls him "vermin."

   D. She says she wants to be doing something else.

35. **Which sentence of dialogue, if added to the passage, would support the conclusion that Mr. Snuggles actually belongs to someone else?**

   A. "What ever possessed me to adopt a cat?"

   B. "You shed on my sheets, you pee on my couch, and now *this*."

   C. "Next time Raul goes out of town, I'm going to babysit his plants instead."

   D. "If you make me late again, I'm going to lose my job. Then how will we eat?"

36. **Which of the following sources should be treated with skepticism even though it is primary?**

   A. An original work of art that has been celebrated and imitated

   B. The research notes of a technician studying infectious diseases

   C. An opinion article by a person who witnessed a famine firsthand

   D. A 1910 article on how to treat measles by an experienced doctor

Read the passages below and answer questions 37-40.

Many people find termites to be destructive little pests, but they are actually ingenious little creatures. If you were to look at a termite mound, you would see first hand how incredible these insects are.

These masters of construction work together to erect high-functioning, green-energy skyscrapers out of nothing but soil, saliva, and dung. The largest one documented is in the Democratic Republic of Congo. This mound, measuring 12.8 meters (41.9 feet) tall, has heat regulation and air conditioning systems. It also contains numerous chambers for food storage, gardens, and babies.

And just think: a termite is only .6 cm long, yet it is still capable of building a sophisticated structure that's 2,013 times its size!

*

As we hiked along the dusty trail deep within the Congo, our tour guide suddenly stopped and held up his hand.

Panic rose inside me, as I expected to see a ghastly hyena or other vicious predator in our midst. But he slowly pointed toward a large mound off the side of the path.

What on earth?

It rose high above us, a tall, sandy structure, its arms outstretched to the sky.

"This," he began in a whisper so as not to disturb its inhabitants, "is a termite mound. Inside are thousands of termites. These tiny little insects have worked together to build this massive structure. And not only is it ventilated to keep them cool, but there are tons of little rooms or chambers inside for different purposes."

WHOA. A termite mound? How on earth did those pesky little bugs do that?

37. **What is the purpose of the first paragraph of Passage 1?**
    A. To inform   C. To persuade
    B. To distract   D. To entertain

38. **What is the primary purpose of Passage 2?**
    A. To inform   C. To persuade
    B. To distract   D. To entertain

39. **With which statement would the author of Passage 1 most likely agree with?**
    A. Things are not always what they seem.
    B. The best things in life come in small packages.
    C. If you try hard enough, you can achieve anything.
    D. Working together accomplishes more than working alone.

40. **The author of Passage 1 supports his/her points primarily by:**
    A. telling humanizing stories.
    B. relying on facts and logic.
    C. pointing to expert sources.
    D. using fear tactics and manipulation.

TABE Practice Exam 1
Answer Key with Explanatory Answers

Section I. Language

1. D. *Perfect* is an adjective that describes the nouns *voice, poise,* and *costume.* **See Lesson: Adjectives and Adverbs**

2. C. The first *early* is an adjective that describes the noun *meeting,* and the second *early* is an adverb that describes the verb *woke.* **See Lesson: Adjectives and Adverbs.**

3. A. May. Months, days, and holidays need to be capitalized, and seasons do not need to be. **See Lesson: Capitalization.**

4. D. *Harry Potter and the Prisoner of Azkaban.* Short prepositions, conjunctions, and articles are not capitalized in publication titles. **See Lesson: Capitalization.**

5. B. *We had a dry summer* and *the crops didn't do well* are independent clauses. **See Lesson: Conjunctions and Prepositions.**

6. D. *On Saturday* is a prepositional phrase. **See Lesson: Conjunctions and Prepositions.**

7. D. The meaning of <u>insatiable</u> in this context is "can't be satisfied." The word "frequently" helps you figure out the meaning of <u>insatiable</u>. **See Lesson: Context Clues and Multiple Meaning Words.**

8. C. The word "channel" has more than one meaning. **See Lesson: Context Clues and Multiple Meaning Words.**

9. A. The meaning of <u>figure</u> in the context of this sentence is "a shape or form." **See Lesson: Context Clues and Multiple Meaning Words.**

10. D. *Their wedding* is a direct object of the verb *plan.* **See Lesson: Direct Objects and Indirect Objects.**

11. C. *The dog* is the direct object of the verb *walk.* **See Lesson: Direct Objects and Indirect Objects.**

12. A. *Snore* is intransitive and cannot take a direct object. **See Lesson: Direct Objects and Indirect Objects.**

13. D. *Who was a year older* describes *Marvin.* **See Lesson: Modifiers.**

14. A. *After reading the book* is a modifier that, by its placement, is incorrectly referenced to *the movie.* The modifier is dangling because there is no noun or pronoun that references the person who read the book. **See Lesson: Modifiers.**

15. C. *That, large,* and *silver* describe *bowl.* **See Lesson: Modifiers, misplaced modifiers, dangling modifiers.**

16. B. To make the word *frog* plural, simply add *-s.* **See Lesson: Nouns.**

17. A. *Supreme Court* is a noun. **See Lesson: Nouns.**

18. B. *Her* is a possessive pronoun. **See Lesson: Pronouns.**

19. B. The relative pronoun *who* introduces a clause that gives more information about the noun *Mrs. Sato.* **See Lesson: Pronouns.**

20. C. *I go to bed early so I do not feel tired.* There should be a comma before so as it is a coordinating conjunction. **See Lesson: Punctuation.**

21. A. *There should be quotation marks.* Direct quotes from someone else should be enclosed in quotation marks. **See Lesson: Punctuation.**

22. B. The root *ami* means "love," so an amicable person would show love or be friendly. **See Lesson: Root Words, Prefixes, and Suffixes.**

23. C. The prefix *in* means "not," so infamous means not known for being famous or for something good, so infamous means notorious. **See Lesson: Root Words, Prefixes, and Suffixes.**

24. A. The root that means "foot" is *ped.* **See Lesson: Root Words, Prefixes, and Suffixes.**

25. A. *Argument* is the only correct spelling. **See Lesson: Spelling.**

26. D. With a word ending in -f, you drop the -f and add -ves. **See Lesson: Spelling.**

27. C. The subject is *Mai and her friend Oksana,* and the predicate is *love to ride roller coasters.* **See Lesson: Subject and Verb Agreement.**

28. A. The subject *he* takes the verb form *is,* not *are.* **See Lesson: Subject and Verb Agreement.**

29. B. This sentence has a predicate within a predicate. The "inside" predicate is *who I have visited for years,* and the "outside" predicate is *my dentist has suddenly disappeared.* **See Lesson: Subject and Verb Agreement.**

30. A. Assertive has a positive connotation. **See Lesson: Synonyms, Antonyms, and Analogies.**

31. A. Quaff is an action that you do with a beverage in the same way that garnish is an action you do with a plate of food. **See Lesson: Synonyms, Antonyms, and Analogies.**

32. B. Adding the prefix "un" would make the word unintentional, which is an antonym for intentional. **See Lesson: Synonyms, Antonyms, and Analogies.**

33. B. Before he went to bed. It is dependent because it does not express a complete thought and relies on the independent clause. The word "before" also signifies the beginning of a dependent clause. **See Lesson: Types of Clauses.**

34. A. She gave her dog a long walk and he slept well that night. These two clauses are of equal grammatical rank and can be connected with a coordinating conjunction. "And" is the conjunction that makes the most sense. **See Lesson: Types of Clauses.**

35. C. Which. The word "which" signifies the beginning of a dependent clause and is the only conjunction that makes sense in the sentence. **See Lesson: Types of Clauses.**

36. C. This is a compound sentence joining two independent clauses with a comma and the conjunction *but*. **See Lesson: Types of Sentences.**

37. D. The subordinate conjunction "because" combines the sentences and puts the focus on Tony preparing for his job interview. **See Lesson: Types of Sentences.**

38. D. This sentence correctly fixes the run-on sentence. **See Lesson: Types of Sentences.**

39. B. *Offered* and *advised* are simple past tense verb forms. **See Lesson: Verbs and Verb Tenses.**

40. A. This is a past tense negative, so it takes the helping verb *did* with the base form *like*. **See Lesson: Verbs and Verb Tenses.**

Section II. Mathematics

1. B. The correct solution is 848.Use the addition algorithm. Carrying will be necessary when adding the digits in the tens place. **See Lesson: Basic Addition and Subtraction.**

2. D. When dividing whole numbers, the remainder is the portion of the dividend left over after finding the whole-number part of the quotient. The remainder is always smaller than the divisor. **See Lesson: Basic Multiplication and Division.**

3. C. Carefully follow the order of operations. First, multiply and divide from left to right. Then, add. **See Lesson: Basic Multiplication and Division.**

$12 \div 4 \times 3 + 1$

$3 \times 3 + 1$

$9 + 1$

10

4. B. The correct solution is 86.54. The radius is 5.25 centimeters and $A = \pi r^2 \approx 3.14(5.25)^2 \approx 3.14(27.5625) \approx 86.54$ square inches. **See Lesson: Circles.**

5. B. The correct solution is 18.84 because $C = \pi d \approx 3.14(6) \approx 18.84$ inches. **See Lesson: Circles.**

6. B. The correct solution is a line. The walls are two planes, and two planes intersect at a line. **See Lesson: Congruence.**

7. B. The correct solution is 2. For a parallelogram, there is rotational symmetry every $180°$. **See Lesson: Congruence.**

8. D. The correct answer is $\frac{3121}{5000}$ because 62.42% as a fraction is $\frac{6242}{10000} = \frac{3121}{5000}$. **See Lesson: Decimals and Fractions.**

9. B. The correct answer is 155% because $1\frac{11}{20}$ as a percent is $1.55 \times 100 = 155\%$. **See Lesson: Decimals and Fractions.**

10. C. The correct solution is −6.

$2x–8 = 5x + 10$	Apply the distributive property.
$–3x–8 = 10$	Subtract $5x$ from both sides of the equation.
$–3x = 18$	Add 8 to both sides of the equation.
$x = –6$	Divide both sides of the equation by $–3$.

See Lesson: Equations with One Variable.

11. D. The correct solution is $x \geq \frac{1}{15}$.

$3x–4(x + 2) \leq 2x + 3 + 12x–12$	Multiply all terms by the least common denominator of 12 to eliminate the fractions.
$3x–4x–8 \leq 2x + 3 + 12x–12$	Apply the distributive property.
$–x–8 \leq 14x–9$	Combine like terms on both sides of the inequality.
$–15x–8 \leq –9$	Subtract $14x$ from both sides of the inequality.
$–15x \leq –1$	Add 8 to both sides of the inequality.
$x \geq \frac{1}{15}$	Divide both sides of the inequality by -15.

See Lesson: Equations with One Variable.

12. D. The correct graph has the two lines intersect at (0, 3). **See Lesson: Equations with Two Variables.**

13. C. The correct solution is (9, 6).

$15x + 5y = 165$	Multiply all terms in the second equation by 5.
$16x = 144$	Add the equations.
$x = 9$	Divide both sides of the equation by 16.
$9–5y = –21$	Substitute 9 in the first equation for x.
$–5y = –30$	Subtract 9 from both sides of the equation.
$y = 6$	Divide both sides of the equation by -5.

See Lesson: Equations with Two Variables.

14. D. If the positive number is 1, then one of its multiples is 3—a prime number. Answer A is therefore false, as is answer C. If the positive number is 0, all of its multiples are 0. Therefore, it has no prime multiples, eliminating answer B. **See Lesson: Factors and Multiples.**

15. B. The correct solution is zip code because it classifies based on location and is a number that does not make sense to average. **See Lesson: Interpreting Categorical and Quantitative Data.**

16. D. The correct solution is the difference between the maximum and minimum is 70 sales. The maximum value is 90, and the minimum value is 20. The difference between these values is 70 sales. **See Lesson: Interpreting Categorical and Quantitative Data.**

17. C. The correct solution is 10 because the difference between boys and girls is 10 participants. **See Lesson: Interpreting Graphics.**

18. B. The correct solution is children's grades because it is dependent on the factors of the parent's education. **See Lesson: Interpreting Graphics.**

19. B. The correct solution is $4,500\pi$ cubic millimeters. The radius is one-half of the diameter, or 15 millimeters. Substitute the values into the formula and simplify using the order of operations, $V = 2 \times \frac{1}{3}\pi r^2 h = 2 \times \frac{1}{3}\pi 15^2(30) = 2 \times \frac{1}{3}\pi(225)(30) = 4,500\pi$ cubic millimeters. **See Lesson: Measurement and Dimension.**

20. B. The correct solution is 588π. Find the radius by substituting in the circumference and dividing by 2π, $14\pi = 2\pi r$; $r = 7$ inches. Substitute the values into the formula and simplify using the order of operations, $V = \pi r^2 h = \pi 7^2(12) = \pi(49)(12) = 588\pi$ cubic inches. **See Lesson: Measurement and Dimension.**

21. B. The correct solution is $1\frac{1}{5}$ because $\frac{2}{5} \times \frac{3}{1} = \frac{6}{5} = 1\frac{1}{5}$. **See Lesson: Multiplication and Division of Fractions.**

22. D. The correct answer is $2\frac{31}{42}$ because $\frac{23}{14} \div \frac{3}{5} = \frac{23}{14} \times \frac{5}{3} = \frac{115}{42} = 2\frac{31}{42}$. **See Lesson: Multiplication and Division of Fractions.**

23. B. The correct solution is $-20x^3y^5$. $-4x^2y^2(5xy^3) = -20x^3y^5$. **See Lesson: Polynomials.**

24. D. The correct solution is $y^3 - 4y^2 + 9y + 3$.

$$(3y^3 - 4y^2 + 6y + 3) - (2y^3 - 3y) = (3y^3 - 4y^2 + 6y + 3) + (-2y^3 + 3y)$$

$$= (3y^3 - 2y^3) - 4y^2 + (6y + 3y) + 3 = y^3 - 4y^2 + 9y + 3$$

See Lesson: Polynomials.

25. C. The correct solution is 8 because 5×10^{-8} is 0.00000005 and 6×10^{-9} is 0.000000006. So, the first cell is about 8 times larger. **See Lesson: Powers, Exponents, Roots, and Radicals.**

26. B. The correct solution is $\frac{81y^6}{x^4}$ because $(9x^{-2}y^3)^2 = 9^2 x^{-2 \times 2} y^{3 \times 2} = 9^2 x^{-4} y^6 = 81 x^{-4} y^6 = \frac{81y^6}{x^4}$. **See Lesson: Powers, Exponents, Roots, and Radicals.**

27. B. To convert 31% to a ratio, note that it is equal to $\frac{31}{100}$, which is 31:100 in colon ratio notation. **See Lesson: Ratios, Proportions, and Percentages.**

28. C. Its vertical speed is 37.5 feet per second. Use the rate-of-change formula to calculate the change in height over the duration of time (change of time):

$$\frac{x_f - x_i}{t_f - t_i} = \frac{30 \text{ feet} - 15 \text{ feet}}{3.6 \text{ s} - 3.2 \text{ s}} = \frac{15 \text{ feet}}{0.4 \text{ s}} = 37.5 \text{ feet per second}$$

See Lesson: Ratios, Proportions, and Percentages.

29. B. The correct solution is 3,600. Substitute the values into the formula and simplify using the order of operations, $A = \frac{1}{2}bh = \frac{1}{2}(90)(80) = 3,600$ square centimeters. **See Lesson: Similarity, Right Triangles, and Trigonometry.**

30. B. The correct solutions are $(-50, 125)$, $(125, -50)$ because adding 175 to the x-coordinate or y-coordinate shows other points of the square. **See Lesson: Similarity, Right Triangles, and Trigonometry.**

31. C. The correct solutions are $-5 \pm \sqrt{35}$.

$x^2 + 10x = 10$	Add 10 to both sides of the equation.
$x^2 + 10x + 25 = 10 + 25$	Complete the square, $\left(\frac{10}{-2}\right)^2 = 5^2 = 25$.
Add 25 to both sides of the equation.	
$x^2 + 10x + 25 = 35$	Simplify the right side of the equation.
$(x + 5)^2 = 35$	Factor the left side of the equation.
$x + 5 = \pm\sqrt{35}$	Apply the square root to both sides of the equation.
$x = -5 \pm \sqrt{35}$	Subtract 5 from both sides of the equation.

See Lesson: Solving Quadratic Equations.

32. C. The correct solutions are -0.88 and -9.13. **See Lesson: Solving Quadratic Equations.**

$x = \frac{-10 \pm \sqrt{10^2 - 4(1)(8)}}{2(1)}$	Substitute 1 for a, 10 for b, and 8 for c.
$x = \frac{-10 \pm \sqrt{100 - 32}}{2}$	Apply the exponent and perform the multiplication.
$x = \frac{-10 \pm \sqrt{68}}{2}$	Perform the subtraction.
$x = \frac{-10 \pm 8.25}{2}$	Apply the square root.
$x = \frac{-10 + 8.25}{2}$, $x = \frac{-10 - 8.25}{2}$	Separate the problem into two expressions.
$x = \frac{-1.75}{2} = -0.88$, $x = \frac{-18.25}{2} = -9.13$	Simplify the numerator and divide.

33. D. The correct solution is 48.6 because $5.4(3)(3) = 48.6$ gallons. **See Lesson: Solving Real-World Mathematical Problems.**

34. A. The correct solution is \$23.05 because the total cost is $18.49(2) + 39.97 = 36.98 + 39.97 = 76.95$. The amount of change is $100 - 76.95 = \$23.05$. **See Lesson: Solving Real-World Mathematical Problems.**

35. C. The correct solution is 8,000 pounds. $4\,T \times \frac{2,000\ lb}{1\ T} = 8,000\ lb$. **See Lesson: Standards of Measure.**

36. A. The correct solution is 0.147 kiloliters. $147\,L \times \frac{1\,kL}{1,000\,L} = \frac{147}{1,000} = 0.147\,kL$. **See Lesson: Standards of Measure.**

37. C. The correct solution is a group of students selected by their after-school availability because the students are only available after school. **See Lesson: Statistical Measures.**

38. A. The correct solution is a researcher interviewing all nurses at all hospitals because this study collects data on every subject within a sample. **See Lesson: Statistical Measures.**

39. C. The correct solution is $\frac{3}{10}$. There are three options, 3, 6, and 9, out of 10, making the probability $\frac{3}{10}$. **See Lesson: Statistics & Probability: The Rules of Probability.**

40. B. The correct solution is $0.38. The probability for each event is

Prize	$100	$1,000	$10,000	$100,000	Not Winning
Probability	1 in 500 = 0.002	1 in 25,000 = 0.00004	1 in 100,000 = 0.00001	1 in 2,500,000 = 0.0000004	0.9799496

The expected value is $0.002(100) + 0.00004(1,000) + 0.00001(10,000) + 0.0000004(100,000) + 0.9799496(0) = 0.2 + 0.04 + 0.1 + 0.04 + 0 = \$0.38$. **See Lesson: Statistics & Probability: The Rules of Probability.**

Section III. Reading

1. C. The main point of this paragraph is that science fiction often depicts a particular kind of post-apocalyptic survival scenario that would not work in fact. The title of the passage should reflect this idea. **See Lesson: Evaluating and Integrating Data.**

2. C. The author argues that the New York City subway system would not be a good place to take refuge after a major weather event if nobody were working to pump the water out. Information about the water would help illustrate that point. **See Lesson: Evaluating and Integrating Data.**

3. C. Sidebar information should be peripheral to the text. That means it's clearly related and interesting to the same audience. Here, the list of sci-fi novels would be the best option. **See Lesson: Evaluating and Integrating Data.**

4. A. If Carla wants to limit her calorie intake, she needs to know not only how many calories are in a serving of the foods and drinks she consumes, but also the number of servings per package or bottle. **See Lesson: Evaluating and Integrating Data.**

5. D. The passage states explicitly that the idea of raising children in prison is controversial, so this is not an assumption. It does assume that our society should attempt to help children born to mothers in prison. **See Lesson: Facts, Opinions, and Evaluating an Argument.**

6. C. The main argument in this passage is that it may be beneficial to both mothers and babies if women who give birth in prison are allowed to keep their children with them. One assumption behind the passage is that society must promote the health and safety of children, but this is not the main argument. **See Lesson: Facts, Opinions, and Evaluating an Argument.**

7. B. The statement makes a factual statement about how people said they felt. This makes it a fact even though it contains opinion information. **See Lesson: Facts, Opinions, and Evaluating an Argument.**

8. B. The argument that prison nursery programs can be beneficial is an opinion statement because it makes a judgment. **See Lesson: Facts, Opinions, and Evaluating an Argument.**

9. D. I gotta go to school. It is the sentence that uses the most slang. **See Lesson: Formal and Informal Language.**

10. B. A football game. A stadium is an informal setting where formal language is not necessary. **See Lesson: Formal and Informal Language.**

11. A. At brunch. It is an informal setting that a person goes to with their friends. **See Lesson: Formal and Informal Language.**

12. B. I am writing to explain my business plan. The sentence does not have any contractions and uses the most polite and formal vocabulary. **See Lesson: Formal and Informal Language.**

13. C. The topic of this paragraph is related to obesity, but it is more narrowly focused on the fad diets people use as they try to control their weight. **See Lesson: Main Ideas, Topic Sentences, and Supporting Details.**

14. A. The first sentence of this paragraph leads the reader toward the main idea, which is expressed next in a topic sentence about the harmfulness of fad diets. **See Lesson: Main Ideas, Topic Sentences, and Supporting Details.**

15. C. A description of a failed experience with fad diets would function as a supporting detail in this paragraph about the negative consequences of fad diets. **See Lesson: Main Ideas, Topic Sentences, and Supporting Details.**

16. B. Although this description of the paragraph would be valid in an opinion response, it is not merely a statement of the main idea because it adds the reader's judgment about the paragraph. **See Lesson: Main Ideas, Topic Sentences, and Supporting Details.**

17. A. Although a statistic about early childhood obesity might belong in a passage focusing on obesity rates, it would be off-topic information in this paragraph on the harm of fad dieting. **See Lesson: Main Ideas, Topic Sentences, and Supporting Details.**

18. B. There is only one arrow leading from the start box, and it goes to the "look in the kitchen" box. **See Lesson: Summarizing Text and Using Text Features.**

19. D. The arrow that is labeled "No" directs readers to "Look in the kitchen." **See Lesson: Summarizing Text and Using Text Features.**

20. D. The pie chart indicates the amount of time students of different genders contribute to discussions. The larger wedge for male speaking indicates that 70% of class discussion time is dominated by male speakers. **See Lesson: Summarizing Text and Using Text Features.**

21. B. If you read the labels carefully, you will see that the bar graph shows how many times students of each gender *are interrupted* during class discussions. The graph shows that students are interrupted more often than male students. **See Lesson: Summarizing Text and Using Text Features.**

22. B. The data in the chart and graph could help show that male students are receiving more chances to speak in class discussions, and that it would be a good idea to increase gender parity. **See Lesson: Summarizing Text and Using Text Features.**

23. B. The tone of this letter is hostile and arrogant as the author openly assumes her wealth and influence will secure a good chemistry grade for her daughter. **See Lesson: Tone and Mood, Transition Words.**

24. C. The author of the letter uses mostly polite language to make her arrogant request, but her language becomes openly hostile when she calls grading practices "petty" and accuses Dr. Rodriguez of being "incompetent." **See Lesson: Tone and Mood, Transition Words.**

25. A. A teacher receiving a note like this would likely feel furious. **See Lesson: Tone, Mood, and Transition Words.**

26. C. The phrase "in fact" adds emphasis to the writer's implicit point that she intends to make sure her daughter unfairly receives a high chemistry grade. **See Lesson: Tone, Mood, and Transition Words.**

27. D. A transition between these two sentences would likely suggest contrast. Good choices would be words like *nevertheless* or *however*. **See Lesson: Tone, Mood, and Transition Words**

28. C. The paragraph is meant to convince the reader to pay for or otherwise help with the cleanup of Fly Lake. This makes it a persuasive text. **See Lesson: Types of Passages, Text Structures, Genre and Theme.**

29. B. The paragraph points out a problem at the beginning and offers a solution. In between, it describes the environmental problems at Fly Lake in a logical order. **See Lesson: Types of Passages, Text Structures, Genre and Theme.**

30. A. The author of this text is expressing a point of view in a short-form piece. This is most likely an essay. **See Lesson: Types of Passages, Text Structures, Genre and Theme.**

31. B. When finding a theme, steer away from options that only reflect a sentence or two, and from options that are not fully supported by the whole text. The entire passage makes an argument for cleaning up a polluted site because it would benefit everyone. **See Lesson: Types of Passages, Text Structures, Genre and Theme.**

32. A. Adelia is attempting to call a pet, not a child. You can infer this because she calls Mr. Snuggles "vermin" and bangs on a bowl with a spoon to get his attention. **See Lesson: Understanding Primary Sources, Making Inferences, and Drawing Conclusions.**

33. B. Adelia's bathrobe is not evidence that she is frustrated at Mr. Snuggles. **See Lesson: Understanding Primary Sources, Making Inferences, and Drawing Conclusions.**

34. A. Adelia tries repeatedly to call Mr. Snuggles, and when he does not come, she goes out to look for him. This implies that she does care about him, even if she is angry at him. **See Lesson: Understanding Primary Sources, Making Inferences, and Drawing Conclusions.**

35. C. The line about Raul and his plants does not explicitly say Adelia is babysitting Mr. Snuggles, but it suggests that she is caring for the pet for someone else. **See Lesson: Understanding Primary Sources, Making Inferences, and Drawing Conclusions.**

36. D. A 1910 article on medicine is highly outdated. Even if the writer is an experienced doctor, the advice presented would likely not be worth following. **See Lesson: Understanding Primary Sources, Making Inferences, and Drawing Conclusions.**

37. C. Passage 1 is intended to persuade readers that termites are amazing insects. **See Lesson: The Author's Purpose and Point of View.**

38. D. Passage 2 tells a story, which is meant to entertain. **See Lesson: The Author's Purpose and Point of View.**

39. A. Passage 1 says, "Many people find termites to be destructive little pests, but they are actually ingenious little creatures." This suggests that termites are misunderstood and things are not always what they seem. **See Lesson: The Author's Purpose and Point of View.**

40. B. The author of Passage 1 uses primarily facts and logic, although she could strengthen her points by clearly identifying sources or establishing her credentials. **See Lesson: The Author's Purpose and Point of View.**